The
Hot Dog
Cookbook

"The Hot Dog Cookbook is a tailgater's dream. Whether getting ready for a baseball or football game or just relaxing at a backyard barbecue, this cookbook better be on the guest list."

—Bob Wood, author of *Dodger Dogs to Fenway Franks*

The
Hot Dog
Cookbook

The Wiener Work the World Awaited

by

Jess M. Brallier

(self-confessed hot dog junkie)

with a foreword by the author's mother

The Globe Pequot Press

Old Saybrook, Connecticut

Text design by Nancy Freeborn
Illustrations by James Ennis Kirkland

Library of Congress Cataloging-in-Publication Data
Brallier, Jess M.
    The hot dog cookbook : the wiener work the world awaited/by Jess M. Brallier.—1st ed.
       p. cm.
    ISBN 1-56440-291-6
    1. Cookery (Frankfurters) I. Title.
TX749.B724 1993
641.6'62—dc20
                                    93-24604
                                      CIP

Manufactured in the United States of America
First Edition/Second Printing

To
Adam and Melissa
Beth and Becca
Jess and Laurie

Contents

PART I

Hot Dog History

PART II

Recipes

Foreword

JUNIOR'S ALWAYS BEEN A GOOD BOY. I'm not at all surprised that he's gone and written this hot dog cookbook. One day—he probably wasn't much more than two or two-and-a-half—when I tried to play house with him (my neighbor Flo, the one with all those noisy girls, had given us an old toy kitchen) well, when I asked for a cup of tea, he instead brought me a toy hot dog between two plastic pancakes. And then when I asked for a cookie, he brought me a milk bottle with another toy hot dog jammed into the bottle. I turned to my sister, Betty—she was visiting from Cleveland like she did every spring—and said, "That boy's going to write a hot dog cookbook someday." So I'm not surprised. Not at all.

In school, he was always doing reports on hot dogs. The first one he did was in fourth grade. He did that one in crayon—except for the title: "Our Friend the Hot Dog." He wrote that in ketchup, using one of those squirty bottles like they have in diners. What a mess! I had to throw it out after two days—it stunk to high heaven!

Then he moved on to more serious sorts of reports. In sixth grade he did "The Importance of the Hot Dog in the American Labor Movement: From Samuel Gompers to Oscar Mayer." That won an award from the Iron and Steelworkers Local. And for a junior high English class, he wrote something called "The Hot Dog As Metaphor." I sent that one to Betty in Tampa—she left Cleveland when she married for the third time—with a note that said, "See? Junior's going to write a hot dog cookbook some day. I just know he's gonna."

After high school, Junior wanted to major in hot dog but couldn't find any college with such a thing, not even one of those "ivy" ones. So he went off to New York City, where he started hanging out on street corners—"not to be a ruffian or anything, Ma," he wrote, "but because that's where all the hot dogs are in this city."

Just a year or so ago, Junior's letters to me started asking for things like my favorite hot dog recipes and the secret ingredient for my special hot dog topping and other stuff like, "Dear Mom: Just wondering—when you used to make that hot dog salad that Uncle Freddy liked so much, what pasta did you use—spirals? egg noodles? or just good old elbow macaroni?" So I wrote to Betty and told her that I just knew that Junior must be having serious talks with one of those big fancy eastern book publishers. I remember wondering if that Bennett Cerf man was still alive, because he was obviously pretty smart—you could just tell that from the way he always asked questions on "What's My Line?" Betty warned me to stay *out* of Junior's hot dog book business just the way I stayed out of his hot dog reports in fourth grade. And I did.

Well, look at what happened! I'm *in* Junior's hot dog book! Turned out that the Cerf man was dead, but this other fancy eastern book publisher that Junior ended up with asked me to write this foreword to the book.

So, Dear Reader, I hope you like the book as much as I like Junior and even half as much as he likes hot dogs.

Bon appetit!

The author's mother
Pittsburgh, Pennsylvania

PART I

Hot Dog History

THE HOT DOG WE KNOW AND LOVE was not suddenly invented one Tuesday afternoon in an R&D laboratory by a famous scientist like Edwin Land, J. Robert Oppenheimer, or Dr. Frankenstein. No, not at all. Instead, like similar major movements throughout history and culture, the hot dog was developed and perfected over generations, throughout hundreds of years, and across several continents.

Sometimes it just takes that much work and time if something's really going to be good. Let's start at the beginning.

First, the Sausage

The Babylonians came up with the original concept over 3,500 years ago—one day they decided to stuff spiced meat into animal intestines. This is the sort of thing that when you look back on it, seems so obvious.

Other civilizations adopted and modified the sausage (with their usual flair for the understated, the Greeks called it *orya*). And because the ninth-century B.C. Greek poet Homer praised the sausage (i.e., the hot dog) in his epic *The Odyssey,* his work is now included in the core first-year curriculum of all major universities.

The Romans, whose army marched on its stomach (saved a bundle on shoes!), loved the sausage. It is mentioned in the oldest-known Roman cookbook, dated A.D. 228 (out of print). They called it *salsus*—which ultimately became *sausage* (mumbling was big back then).

Second, the Wiener

Over the next 1,000 years, the popularity of sausages spread like a disease throughout Europe. By the Middle Ages, they began to take on regional characteristics; their shape and size varied from country to country, and local creations were named for the towns

in which they originated. Thus, Austria gave birth to the "Vienna sausage" or wiener-wurst, from which the term *wiener* is derived.

This quirky little practice of nomenclature found its way across the rough seas of the Atlantic and through the dangerous wilderness of our nation's early pioneering years, so that today one finds, for example:

The Chicago Dog—served with yellow mustard, dark green relish, chopped raw onion, tomato slices, and topped with a dash of celery salt on a poppy seed bun.

The Kansas City Dog—a Reuben dog, served with sauerkraut and melted Swiss cheese on a sesame seed roll.

New York City Dogs—plump hot dogs with steamed onions and a pale yellow mustard sauce, sold by street vendors.

The Southern Slaw Dog—in the South they say "drag it through the garden." The slaw is made from chopped cabbage, onions, mayonnaise, spices, and a touch of carrot for color.

Next, the Frankfurter

The modern hot dog—the frankfurter—is descended from a spiced, smoked, slightly curved, thin sausage developed in Frankfurt, Germany.

According to German lore of the pre-Berlin Wall type, the shape of this frankfurter was a tribute to a popular pet dachshund that belonged to a local butcher. The result: by the 1850s, it was commonly called a "dachshund sausage." It was customarily eaten with sauerkraut and mustard—but no bun (thus the reputation Germans of the 1850s had for being somewhat messy).

In the 1890s, a German immigrant named Charles Feltman began selling dachshund sausages on the street (actually alongside the curb) on New York state's Coney Island (so named by early Dutch settlers because the area was overrun with rabbits, or "coneys"). Feltman became so successful that he was able to open a frankfurter restaurant—the first in the United States.

Today, one hundred years later, on that same Coney Island, more than 100,000 hot dogs are eaten on a single summer weekend. And Nathan's, the trademark New York eatery that also began on the boardwalk at Coney Island, averages sales of over *$70 million* per year.

Then, the Bun

The development of America's favorite food took a large step forward when in 1904, at the St. Louis World's Fair's Louisiana Purchase Exposition, another Frankfurt native innocently began selling dachshund sausages: *Not only did his mere presence at the exposition popularize the food nationwide, but this entrepreneur improved the package by introducing the bun.*

Here's how: Gloves were customarily supplied for customers to wear while eating their frankfurters. But at the fair, too many people walked away still wearing them; the vendor soon ran out of spare gloves. In desperation, he convinced a nearby baker to make frank-shaped rolls as a substitute for gloves. The rolls actually worked better, and a new tradition was born.

At Last, the Hot Dog

The term *hot dog* was coined in 1906 at a football game (although some hot dog historians insist it was a baseball game) at New York's Polo Grounds. Sold from a tank that kept them heated, their vendors called out, "Get your red hot dachshund dogs!"

Inspired by the phrase, sports cartoonist Tad Dorgan went back to his office and began sketching a cartoon based on the notion of a real dachshund in a bun, covered with mustard. But up against deadline and realizing he couldn't spell "dachshund," Dorgan—as is typical of any of the New York-based media sort—settled for "hot dog."

Only a quarter of a century—one score and five years—later, ex-vaudevillians Neil and Carl Fletcher invented the Corn Dog (a wiener-on-a-stick dipped in corn batter and deep fried) in Dallas, Texas.

Now the hot dog industry was advancing by leaps and bounds, so much so that by 1939, President Franklin D. Roosevelt was serving hot dogs (and beer!) to King George VI.

Nowadays

As the twenty-first century dawns, the hot dog has secured the sort of popularity this remarkable food surely deserves:

● *During the next twenty-four hours*—just like any average day over the past twenty-five years—fifty million hot dogs will be consumed in the United States.

● *This year*, the average American will eat between 80 and 100 hot dogs.

● In fact, *from Memorial Day to Labor Day*, Americans enjoy more than five billion hot dogs (laid end to end, that's enough to encircle the globe more than fifteen times!).

The hot dog's popularity is, without a doubt, widespread, ranging from sea to sea, from Mexico to the Arctic, from the inner city to the jovial countryside, even to Europe, the Far East, and *the moon* (NASA approved the hot dog as a regular menu item on all the Apollo moon flights and *Skylab* missions—they've been a real favorite on all space-shuttle travels). The hot dog cares not a bit what your annual income or street address might be, or your color or sex; it asks only that you eat it. So not only does the hot dog taste great, but it is also politically correct, the perfect food for the turn of the century.

● On March 11, 1992, *The New York Times* Living Section declared the hot dog— along with apple pie and salsa—the "new mainstream."

So welcome to the perfect book—the very Bible!—for the newfound mainstream. With this book you can lead a movement (or at least cause one); entertain friends and foes alike; and bring the spirit of America back to your neighborhood with friendly backyard celebrations featuring dishes that surprise, amaze, fulfill, entertain, satisfy, and sometimes even *shock*. You'll be a hit at both the home (your kids will beam with pride) and the office (you'll probably get promoted).

Go for it! . . . and remember, God bless America.

PART II

Recipes

Boffo Breakfasts

When you think how easily most people order ham, bacon, or any variety of boring sausage for breakfast, it's downright shocking how few demand a hot dog dish to get the day started.

Some have speculated that the fault might lie with the owners and managers of the nation's diners and fast-food outlets and not with open-minded consumers like you, me, and Don Ho. Mr. Ho, the very popular Hawaiian entertainer, is known for eating dogs for breakfast. Ho boils his franks in a mixture of water, garlic powder, chopped onion, and soy sauce. Then he slices them diagonally into three or four pieces and places them on top of pork and beans over steamed rice. He covers that with a coat of gravy and serves it with a side dish of scrambled eggs with green onions.

It's no wonder that the guy is so popular.

Felix's Franks 'n Eggs

Suggestion: serve with [beer] and french fries

2 tablespoons margarine (healthier than butter)
2 hot dogs, sliced
1 scallion, chopped
4 eggs, beaten severely
4 tablespoons whole milk (skim's healthier but puts the whole dish at some risk)
salt and pepper, to taste
1 tablespoon chopped parsley
ketchup

1. In a skillet, melt the margarine; then sauté the dogs and scallions for a couple of minutes.

2. Meanwhile, beat together the eggs, milk, salt, and pepper and pour into skillet, covering the dogs and onions. Cook, stirring, until eggs are the way you like them.

3. Sprinkle with parsley, and serve with ketchup on the side.

Makes 2 servings.

"Some people don't salivate when they walk by a hot dog stand and smell that great symbol of American cuisine, bursting with grease and salt. But they are a very, very small group."

—*The New York Times*

The Official Eiffel Tower Hot Dog Quiche

Suggestion: serve with

9-inch baked pie shell
½ pound chopped hot dogs
1 ½ cups grated Cheddar or Swiss cheese
½ cup chopped scallions (preferred) or onion
4 eggs
3 tablespoons flour
1 ½ cups whole milk
¼ teaspoon dry mustard

1. Cover bottom of crust with hot dogs, and carefully arrange the cheese and scallions over them.

2. Beat together the eggs, flour, milk, and dry mustard, and pour over the dogs and cheese.

3. Bake at 350° for 30 to 40 minutes or until set.

Makes 6 servings.

THE HOT DOG AS AN *INTERNATIONAL* PHENOMENON

The favorite meal of Marlene Dietrich, the *internationally* famous actress, was hot dogs and champagne.

Frank's Favorite Frankfurter Frittata

Suggestion: serve with

> More hot dogs—2 million a year—are sold at Chicago's O'Hare International Airport than at any other single location in the world.

6 tablespoons margarine (may substitute butter)
large onion, thinly sliced
½ chopped green pepper
4 hot dogs shredded
6 eggs, beaten
½ cup grated Parmesan cheese
¼ cup chopped parsley
1 teaspoon salt
¼ teaspoon Tabasco
¼ teaspoon Worcestershire

1. Melt the margarine in an iron (or other ovenproof) skillet and sauté the onion and green pepper until the onions just begin to brown.

2. Add the hot dogs and cook until lightly browned.

3. Combine the eggs with the Parmesan cheese, parsley, and seasonings; pour over the dogs and cook until eggs are set.

4. Place under the broiler for a few minutes to lightly brown the top.

5. Cut into wedges and serve.

Makes 4 servings.

Becca's Breakfast Casserole from Charleston

Suggestion: serve with

4 hot dogs, sliced
1 medium onion, thinly sliced
1 cup grated Cheddar cheese
1 egg
1 cup whole milk
½ teaspoon dry mustard
dash of Worcestershire
1 cup flour
1 teaspoon baking powder
1 teaspoon salt

1. Put dogs, onions, and cheese in bottom of buttered 1½-quart shallow casserole.

2. In a bowl, beat together the egg, milk, dry mustard, and Worcestershire.

3. Sift together flour, baking powder, and salt. Add to the egg mixture and blend nicely. Pour over dogs.

4. Bake at 375° for 25 minutes or until golden brown.

Makes 4 servings.

> The most frequent servers of hot dogs are women ages twenty-five to forty-four who are married, have young children, and live in small towns and rural areas throughout the Southeast.

McDogs

Suggestion: serve with 🍺

2 English muffins
1 hot dog
2 eggs
2 slices American cheese

1. Toast English muffins and keep warm in oven.

2. Saute hot dog in skillet until brown; slice in half lengthwise and then in half crosswise. Divide the hot dog evenly onto two English muffin halves.

3. Poach or fry the eggs and lay on top of hot dogs.

4. Top with cheese and place under broiler until cheese melts. Top with remaining English muffin halves.

Makes 2 servings.

In 1957, the United States Chamber of Commerce officially designated July as National Hot Dog Month.

Hors d'Oeuvres

Many have said that appetizers (i.e., hors d'oeuvres) are the essential key to successful entertaining and accelerated social climbing—after all, it's the old story of "first impressions make lasting impressions."

For example, if you have the boss and her husband over for the evening and you make some wonderful hot dog dish (see later, "Lunches, Dinners, and Midnight Snacks") but start the visit off with an awful appetizer that smells like fish or has no flair or presentation, you can forget a promotion or raise, at least for fourteen months. The same goes for your child's intended or the future in-laws or even your new probation officer. All of these social occasions demand sure-fire, top-of-the-line hors d'oeuvres.

Always remember: (1) hot dogs come already cooked, so preparing these tasty treats gives you time to clean the powder room or take a quick nap; and (2) presentation, presentation, and presentation—your hors d'oeuvres tray can take on the subtle hues and brilliant tones of a Renaissance painting by the simple addition of olives, parsley, cheese, pimientos, and Oreos.

So when it comes to entertaining, play it safe and go with hot dogs.

Tube Steak Pâté

Suggestion: serve with

1 hot dog (make darn sure this one's an all-beef hot dog)
1 teaspoon sweet relish
2 green olives, pimientos left in
8 saltine crackers
mayonnaise
pepper

1. Rev up the blender to full speed and drop in hot dog.

2. Add relish and olives.

3. Run the blender at high speed for 90 seconds.

4. Spread the saltine crackers generously with mayonnaise.

5. Spread pâté on crackers; add pepper to taste.

Makes 8 servings.

THE HEALTHY HOT DOG

Feature #1

■

The official Weight Watchers diet regimen includes hot dogs.

Beth's Hot Dog Bagel Betchas

Suggestion: serve with

4 hot dogs
¼ cup grated sharp Cheddar cheese
¼ cup condensed tomato soup
1 tablespoon grated onion
½ teaspoon horseradish
¼ teaspoon prepared mustard
¼ teaspoon Worcestershire sauce
16 mini bagels, toasted

1. Chop the hot dogs and place in a mixing bowl. Add the Cheddar cheese, tomato soup, grated onion, horseradish, mustard, and Worcestershire and stir it all up well.

2. Spread on toasted mini bagels. Place on a cookie sheet and broil 6 inches from the heat for 5 minutes or so, until they get bubbly and lightly browned.

Makes 16 servings.

When something as good as the hot dog comes along, everybody wants to take credit. For example, in 1987, the civic leaders of Frankfurt, Germany, celebrated the 500th birthday of the hot dog in that city, claiming that the frankfurter was developed there in

keep going →

Tea Sandwiches

Suggestion: serve with 🍺 and tea

4 hot dogs
1 cucumber
⅓ cup mayonnaise (homemade preferred)
½ teaspoon minced fresh dill
12 slices white bread, crusts removed

1. Chop the hot dogs fine.
2. Peel the cucumber and cut in half lengthwise. With a spoon, scrape out the seeds and throw them away. Chop the cucumber fine.
3. Combine hot dogs, cucumber, mayonnaise, and dill and mix well.
4. Spread on six slices of bread; top each with remaining bread slices.
5. Cut into triangles and arrange artistically on a tray.

Makes 24 little sandwiches.

1484, five full years before Christopher Columbus set sail for the New World. Yet the leading residents of Vienna (Wien), Austria, insist upon pointing to the term *wiener* as legitimate proof of their long-held claim to being the birthplace of the hot dog. I had a phys-ed

keep going ➝

Deviled Eggs

Suggestion: serve with BEER

6 hard-boiled eggs, peeled and chilled
¼ cup mayonnaise
2 hot dogs, finely chopped
1 teaspoon curry powder
¼ teaspoon dry mustard
freshly ground pepper
paprika
sprigs of parsley

1. Cut the eggs in half lengthwise; remove the yolks, put in a mixing bowl, and mash with a fork.

2. To the smashed yolks, add the mayonnaise, hot dogs, curry powder, mustard, and pepper and mix real well.

3. Mound the mixture into the egg-white halves and chill for 1 hour before serving. Top with paprika and garnish attractively with parsley sprigs.

Makes 12 servings.

teacher in eighth grade who once instructed my class (while substituting for our unmarried but pregnant world history teacher) that it was this hot dog controversy that initiated the outbreak of World War I. I was the only class member who found the theory fascinating.

THE END

Martini Dogs

Suggestion: serve with ![beer bottle] (or martinis)

about 30 large pimiento-stuffed olives
3 hot dogs
1 3-ounce package cream cheese, at *room temperature*
a drop or 2 of Tabasco

1. With a steady hand, cut the stuffed olives in half lengthwise. Remove the pimiento stuffing and put pimientos in a chopping bowl (a solid mixing bowl will also do the trick) along with the hot dogs.

2. Chop the hot dogs and pimiento until coarse.

3. Add the cream cheese to the dogs and pimiento and mix. Add the Tabasco and mix one more time.

4. Fill the olive halves with the mixture and fasten with colored cocktail picks.

5. Chill in the refrigerator for at least 1 hour before serving.

Makes 6 servings.

Let's face it: Hot dogs sound funny, feel odd, and hell, yes, even look obscene.

Adam's Atomic Appetizer

Suggestion: serve with

6 hard-boiled eggs, peeled
6 tablespoons mayonnaise (store-bought or homemade)
½ teaspoon Tabasco sauce
¼ teaspoon dry mustard
Ritz crackers
½ pound hot dogs, sliced thin

1. Chop hard-boiled eggs and mix with mayonnaise and seasonings.

2. Spread on Ritz crackers, top with hot dog rounds, and serve.

Makes enough, depending on time of day.

A LITERARY FEATURE:

"The Hot Dog as a Meatball Metaphor"

Making hot dogs might be compared to making meatballs. Instead of shaping seasoned meat into balls, it is formed into the traditional hot dog shape by using casings, which are removed prior to packaging.

Barbecued Cocktail Franks

Suggestion: serve with 🍺

1 small onion, grated
2 cups of your favorite store-bought barbecue sauce
1 pound cocktail franks

1. Combine onion, barbecue sauce, and franks in saucepan and heat through.

2. Thin with a little water (or beer), if necessary.

3. Serve the sauce hot, in a nice little bowl, alongside a plate of the cocktail franks—and don't forget toothpicks!

Makes 8 servings.

The Making of an Oscar Mayer *(for example)* Hot Dog

Oscar Mayer makes hot dogs in an *electronically* controlled continuous process that takes just forty-five minutes from fresh meat to vacuum-sealed package. The unique system is dubbed "Hot Dog Highway" because the links move along twelve high-speed lanes, "bumper to bumper," at the rate of 38,000

continued ➞

Bob's Currant Dogs

Suggestion: serve with

1 pound cocktail franks
1–2 tablespoons Coleman's dry mustard
1 cup currant jelly

1. Simmer franks until hot.

2. Mix the mustard and currant jelly, making a sauce. This is your shot to call—make it as "mustardly" as you (or your guests) can stand.

3. Combine the sauce and hot dogs in something appropriate and serve with toothpicks.

Makes 6 servings.

per hour. The meat is finely chopped, seasoned, and stuffed into cellulose casings, then linked, smoked, roasted, and chilled. Without a pause, the casings are removed, and the hot dogs are vacuum-sealed in a Zip-lock, "twin pack" of transparent, airtight plastic. Then, for customer convenience, nutritional information and a toll-free 800-number are added to each package.

Bourbon Dogs

Suggestion: serve with

1 pound cocktail franks
2 cups ketchup
¾ cup dark brown sugar
¾ cup bourbon
2 tablespoons minced onion
½ cup spring water

1. Combine everything and simmer for 30 or so minutes in saucepan.

2. Serve with toothpicks.

Makes 8 servings.

In May 1983, a 1,983-foot-long hot dog was made by Bill-Mar Foods of Zeeland, Wisconsin.

Wieners à la Fruited Brandy Sauce

Suggestion: serve with

1 can beef broth

1 9-ounce can crushed pineapple

⅓ cup currants

2 tablespoons cornstarch

¼ cup spring or tap water

½ cup brandy (or ⅔ cup depending on whom you're serving)

12 hot dogs

1. Place the broth, crushed pineapple with juice, and currants in a saucepan over moderate heat.

2. Mix the cornstarch with the water. When the broth begins to bubble, add the cornstarch and cook until thickened and transparent, stirring constantly. Remove from heat and stir in the brandy.

3. Place the hot dogs in a shallow baking dish. Pour the sauce over the hot dogs and place in a 375˚ oven for 8 minutes or until heated through. Serve with toothpicks and pride.

Makes 6 servings.

In 1978, a 6-foot-long, 681-pound all-beef hot dog in a 100-pound poppy seed bun lathered with two gallons of mustard was served by David Berg of Chicago.

Wiener Canapés

Suggestion: serve with 🍺

6 hot dogs
¾ cup grated sharp Cheddar cheese
½ teaspoon Worcestershire sauce
¼ cup finely chopped onion
1 egg, beaten
1 teaspoon Dijon-style mustard
36 crackers or slices of party rye

1. Chop hot dogs fine. Take a break and then add remaining ingredients (except the crackers or party rye) and mix thoroughly.

2. Spread on crackers or slices of party rye.

3. Place in 375° oven for about 15 minutes, or until cheese melts and the tops are lightly browned.

Makes 36 canapés.

If hot dogs are slashed at random they will curl into fun shapes as they heat—great for a Freddy Kreuger theme party!

Ruby's Munchkernickles

Suggestion: serve with

6 hot dogs

1 10-ounce can tomato soup

1 cup grated Cheddar cheese

1 teaspoon horseradish

1 teaspoon prepared mustard

48 assorted crackers or toast points (depending on the occasion)

1. In a decent-sized mixing bowl, chop dogs fine and add tomato soup.

2. Stir in grated cheese, horseradish, and mustard and mix well.

3. Spread on crackers or toast and place under broiler until lightly browned.

Makes 48 munchkernickles.

In 1957, when Queen Elizabeth II served hot dogs at a royal banquet held for the American Bar Association, there was speculation as to how the Queen *really* feels about lawyers. Thirty years later, Buckingham Palace still refuses comment on the matter.

Hot Dog and Olive Spread

Suggestion: serve with

½ cup pimiento-stuffed olives, chopped
6 hot dogs, finely chopped
½ cup store-bought mayonnaise
½ teaspoon dry mustard
pita bread triangles

1. Mix first four ingredients thoroughly in a bowl and spread on pita bread triangles.

2. Broil until lightly browned.

Makes about 24.

Hot dogs are an economical buy. A pound of wieners yields a pound of edible food, with virtually no weight loss during preparation.

Peanut Rollies

Suggestion: serve with  (at your your own risk . . . there's just something about beer and peanut butter)

6 slices of soft white bread
½ cup chunky peanut butter
6 hot dogs, cut in half lengthwise
Pam (you know, like in the spray can)

1. Remove crusts from bread and cut bread in half diagonally.

2. Spread each triangle with peanut butter.

3. Place ½ dog on bread. Bring up the two corners of bread and fasten with toothpick.

4. Spray the outside of each roll-up with Pam.

5. Broil about 6 inches from heat until golden brown.

Makes 12 hors d'oeuvres.

Frankly Fondue

Suggestion: serve with

1 garlic clove, peeled
8 hot dogs, cut into 1-inch pieces
½ pound chunk of Swiss cheese, grated (about 2 cups)
1½ teaspoons flour
¾ cup Chablis or sauterne
¼ teaspoon salt
¼ teaspoon dry mustard
⅛ teaspoon nutmeg
2 tablespoons cognac

1. Rub the inside of a chafing dish with the garlic clove.

2. Cook hot dogs first, then spear with toothpicks and place in chafing dish to keep warm.

3. Toss the cheese with the flour and place in a double boiler. Add the wine and stir until melted. Add the salt, mustard, nutmeg, and cognac. When fondue begins to bubble, remove from heat and pour cheese mixture over and around the hot dog pieces. *Serve at once.* Keep the cheese soft and melted over the chafing-dish burner or candle.

Makes about 36 appetizers.

Soups and Salads

When you look at hot dogs with cold logic, there is no reason why they shouldn't augment the flavors of soup. After all, they are pure meat, delicately flavored, with nary a speck of waste. However, be careful—every soup does not lend itself to using hot dogs. Some soups are so strongly flavored that they overwhelm the hot dogs, and we certainly don't want that to happen.

Hot dogs can also do wonders for your salads, health, and children. Forget cold chicken and fish—use hot dogs to really perk up a salad. Also, remember that in the summer most of us are more active than in winter and additional protein is needed to sustain muscles. So become a "protein sneaker" by slipping healthful hot dogs into all your salads, even your neighbor's or mother-in-law's salads when they're not looking. And last, remember that your normal child hates a healthful salad. So stick some chopped-up dogs in there and maybe by chance the kid will consume a piece of carrot, radish, or lettuce, along with the dogs.

With both soups and salads, I suggest you try some of the following recipes first, but then move on to "soup-ing up" your own creations. This cookbook represents, in great part, a publishing program conceived with an interactive intention, i.e., that you would push the world of hot dogs—especially in the soup and salad genres—far beyond the limits of this book.

Melissa's Merrick Wiener Soup

Suggestion: serve with BEER

4 hot dogs

1 onion

2 carrots

1 stalk celery

6 small red potatoes

1/4 pound green beans

1 tablespoon olive oil

1/4 teaspoon thyme

1/4 teaspoon oregano

3 1/2 cups chicken broth

1/2 cup frozen whole kernel corn

1/2 cup elbow macaroni, cooked

3 tablespoons chopped fresh parsley

1/4 teaspoon pepper

salt

1. Slice hot dogs. Chop onion and carrots. Slice celery. Cut potatoes into small cubes. Cut green beans into approximately 1-inch lengths. Rest.

2. Heat olive oil in a soup pot and sauté hot dogs until browned, about 5 minutes. Remove.

3. Add oil, onion, carrots, celery, thyme, and oregano. Cook over medium heat until onion is soft, about 5 minutes.

4. Add broth, 1 cup water, and the potatoes and bring to a boil. Reduce heat and simmer until potatoes are just cooked, about 5 minutes.

5. Add green beans and cook 5 minutes. Add corn and macaroni and cook another 5 minutes. Stir in parsley, hot dogs, and 1/4 teaspoon pepper and heat through.

6. Taste for seasoning and add salt and more pepper if needed.

Makes 6 servings.

Patty's Spud Chowder

Suggestion: serve with

1 large onion, chopped
1 tablespoon vegetable oil
1½ pounds Idaho potatoes, peeled and cut into 1-inch cubes
1 small carrot, grated
1 can chicken broth
4 hot dogs, sliced
1 cup whole milk
¼ cup minced fresh parsley

1. Sauté onion in oil.

2. In saucepan, combine onion, potatoes, carrot, and chicken broth and cook until potatoes are soft.

3. Mash it all up and add the dogs and milk. Simmer until the dogs are heated through—but don't boil.

4. Top with parsley and serve.

Makes 4 servings.

Babe Ruth once downed twelve hot dogs between games of a doubleheader.

Beantown Chowder

Suggestion: serve with 🍺

6 hot dogs, cut in ¼-inch slices
2 tablespoons olive oil
½ cup chopped celery
¾ cup chopped onion
¼ cup chopped green pepper
2 16-ounce cans pork and beans

2 8-ounce cans tomato sauce
½ teaspoon salt
¼ teaspoon pepper
1 teaspoon brown sugar
3 tablespoons parsley

1. Place the sliced hot dogs and olive oil in a large soup kettle over moderate heat. Sauté the dogs until they begin to brown.

2. Add the celery, onion, and green pepper and continue to sauté until the onion is limp and transparent.

3. Remove the pieces of pork from the beans and discard (or feed to the real dog). Add the beans (juice and all) to the hot dog mixture.

4. Add the tomato sauce, parsley, salt, pepper, and brown sugar and mix all well. Cook for 5 to 10 minutes longer or until all ingredients are heated through.

Makes 6 to 8 servings.

South Side Soup

Suggestion: serve with

6 slices white bread, toasted lightly
6 eggs, poached until just firm
6 hot dogs, cut into slices
6 cups hot beef stock
¼ cup chopped fresh parsley
3 tablespoons grated Parmesan cheese

1. Place a slice of toast in the bottom of each of six soup bowls and top with a poached egg. Add the hot dog slices around the egg yolk.

2. Pour 1 cup of the boiling hot soup stock over the toast, egg, and hot dog pieces.

3. Sprinkle with parsley and Parmesan cheese.

4. Eat.

5. Make out your will.

Makes 6 servings.

Hot dogs appear daily on the U.S. Army short-order menu and regularly in school lunch programs, hospitals, nursing homes (often as a last meal), and other institutional facilities. The speed and ease of preparation as well as economical and nutritional value make hot dogs a valuable food for such services.

JWB's Barley Soup

Suggestion: serve with

8 hot dogs, thinly sliced
⅔ cup barley
3 cups water
1 28-ounce can tomatoes
1 cup chopped carrots
½ cup chopped onion
½ cup chopped leeks
1 cup chopped turnip
¾ cup chopped celery
¼ cup parsley, finely chopped
salt and freshly grated pepper, to taste

1. Place the dog slices, barley, and water in a saucepan with a tightly fitting cover. Cook over moderate heat for 20 minutes.

2. Add the tomatoes, carrots, onion, turnip, leeks, celery, and parsley and continue to cook over moderate heat for another 40 minutes or until the carrots are soft and tender.

3. Add salt and pepper, to taste.

Makes 6 to 8 servings.

Laurie's Luscious Ligonier Lentil Soup

Suggestion: serve with 🍺

1½ cups lentils

7 cups chicken or beef broth

1 28-ounce can crushed tomatoes, with their juice

1 large onion stuck with 2 cloves

1 bay leaf

½ teaspoon thyme

2 cloves garlic, crushed

salt and pepper, to taste

4 hot dogs, sliced

croutons

1. Wash lentils and place in large soup pot. Add the broth, tomatoes, onion, bay leaf, thyme, and garlic. Bring to a boil, reduce the heat, cover, and simmer for about 1 hour, or until the lentils are tender.

2. Remove the bay leaf and onion and add salt and pepper to taste.

3. Add slices of frankfurters and simmer until franks are heated through. Top with croutons.

Makes 8 to 10 servings.

Rev. Townsend's Split Pea Soup

Suggestion: serve with [BEER] (but not on Sundays or at revival meetings)

1½ cups split peas, washed and picked over

8 cups water or broth

1 large onion, chopped

1 medium carrot, finely grated

1 teaspoon curry powder

3 cloves garlic, crushed

1 bay leaf

1 pound hot dogs

1. Combine the peas with the water and all other ingredients, except the dogs, and bring to a boil.

2. Cover and simmer for 2 hours, stirring occasionally, or until peas are tender.

3. Remove bay leaf.

4. Cool a bit and purée (i.e., put all this into a blender and blend until it's thicker than juice but thinner than mashed potatoes).

5. Add the dogs and simmer, diluting with a bit of water if necessary.

Makes 4 to 6 servings.

Bok Choy and Hot Dogs

Suggestion: serve with

1 large head bok choy (Chinese cabbage)

8 hot dogs, cooked and sliced

4 scallions, thinly sliced

2 teaspoons dry mustard

¼ cup soy sauce

1 teaspoon sesame oil

2 teaspoons rice wine vinegar

1. Shred the cabbage and place in a saucepan with water to cover. Bring to a boil and cook for 1 minute or until slightly wilted. Drain thoroughly.

2. Place hot dogs and cabbage in a large bowl. Combine scallions, mustard, soy sauce, sesame oil, and vinegar and mix well. Pour over the cabbage and dogs and refrigerate for several hours before serving.

Makes 6 servings.

TO COOK HOT DOGS FOR SALAD

Place the hot dogs in a sauce pan and cover with water. Cook over moderate heat until the water barely reaches the boiling point. Remove from the heat and let stand for 5 minutes.

Hot Dog Apple Salad

Suggestion: serve with [beer bottle]

6 hot dogs

2 cups elbow macaroni, cooked and drained

4 medium apples (McIntosh recommended)

2 tablespoons lemon juice

4 stalks celery

1 tablespoon finely chopped onion

1 teaspoon celery seed

¼ cup parsley, finely chopped

1 cup sour cream

½ teaspoon salt

1 teaspoon prepared mustard

1. Cut the hot dogs into small cubes. Add to the macaroni and mix well.

2. Peel and core the apples and chop. Add lemon juice and set aside for 5 minutes; then add to the macaroni mixture.

3. Chop the celery and add to the macaroni mixture. Add the chopped onion, celery seed, and parsley. Mix well.

4. In a separate bowl, mix the sour cream, salt, and mustard until well blended. Pour this mixture over the dogs-and-macaroni mixture. Mix well and chill in refrigerator for at least 2 hours.

Makes 6 to 8 servings.

Salad on a Shoestring

Suggestion: serve with

6 hot dogs, cooked
¼ cup chopped red onion
1½ cups chopped celery
¼ cup grated raw carrots
4 radishes, chopped
¾ cup blue cheese dressing
1 large can shoestring potatoes

1. Cut the hot dogs into thirds and then cut each third into shoe-string-sized strips, to match the potatoes. Place in a large bowl and add the onion, celery, carrots, radishes, and half of the blue cheese dressing. Toss thoroughly to mix; cover and chill.

2. When ready to serve, add the remainder of the salad dressing and the shoestring potatoes and toss again.

Makes 6 servings.

National Kraut and Frankfurters Week has been celebrated in February for over forty years.

Topsy-Turvey Wiener Salad

Suggestion: serve with BEER

¾ cup chopped but unpeeled Granny Smith apples
1 teaspoon lemon juice
8 hot dogs
1 head iceberg lettuce
½ cup chopped dill pickle
¾ cup pitted, sliced ripe olives
¾ cup Russian dressing

1. Toss the apples with the lemon juice and set aside.

2. Slice each dog into quarters the long way and then cut the quarters in half cross-wise. Each dog will yield 8 strips (feel free to confirm with hand-held calculator). Break the lettuce up into bite-sized pieces and place in a large salad bowl.

3. Combine the apple, dill pickle, and ripe olives with the hot dog strips and add to lettuce.

4. Add Russian dressing and toss thoroughly.

Makes 6 servings.

Ye Olde Spinach Supreme Salad

Suggestion: serve with

1 pound fresh spinach, washed and drained

2 cups cabbage, finely chopped (½ red cabbage and ½ green
   cabbage will give salad a real visual flair)

1 can mandarin oranges

3 radishes, chopped

1 small red onion, thinly sliced

1 tablespoon chopped parsley

salt and pepper

⅓ cup olive oil

¼ cup cider vinegar

4 hot dogs, cooked and diced

¼ cup Roquefort cheese, crumbled

1. Break the spinach into small pieces. Then place in salad bowl along with cabbage, mandarin oranges, radishes, and red onion.

2. Mix the olive oil, vinegar, parsley, salt and pepper; pour over the salad and toss well.

3. Top salad with the dogs and Roquefort cheese.

Makes 6 servings.

Lunches, Dinners, and Midnight Snacks

This is truly the meat (get it?) of this remarkable cookbook. Here are numerous opportunities to be introduced, through a variety of mouth-watering options, to the wonderful world of wieners.

Note the extensive use of vegetables throughout these carefully compiled dishes. Why so many vegetables? Because, simply, hot dogs and vegetables go together like ham and eggs—and better yet, are no less healthful. With the current bounty of canned, fresh, and frozen vegetables, we face opportunities that would overwhelm Christopher Columbus, Thomas Jefferson, and even General Pershing.

So if you want to send your vegetable platter from the "no-thank-you" class to the "may-I-have-seconds?" class, try cooking your veggies with hot dogs.

Honeymoon Delight

Suggestion: serve with

½ pound bacon

2 medium onions, chopped

1 pound hot dogs, sliced

3 large cans kidney beans, drained and rinsed

½ cup molasses

1 small bottle ketchup

3 shakes of Worcestershire

salt and pepper

1. Fry the bacon crisp, and crumble. Reserve 1 tablespoon of the fat.

2. Sauté onions and franks in the bacon drippings. Put all into large saucepan and cook over medium heat. Stir often to prevent sticking—add a little water if necessary.

Makes 6 to 8 servings.

Max's Hot Dogs

Suggestion: serve with

½ onion, chopped (or 2 tablespoons minced dried onion)

2 tablespoons vegetable oil

¾ cup ketchup

¾ cup water

1 tablespoon brown sugar

1 teaspoon prepared mustard

2 1-pound cans sauerkraut

10 or 12 (i.e., about 11) hot dogs

1. Make the sauce first, sautéing the onion in the oil until it's tender, then add the ketchup, water, sugar, and mustard and bring to a boil.

2. Now open the sauerkraut, drain it well, and put it in a big casserole.

3. Slash or slice the hot dogs and arrange them on top, pour on the sauce, and bake, uncovered, at 350° for 30 minutes.

Makes 4 to 6 servings.

for the twelve Wienermobile driver slots. Mathematically, it is actually easier to become president of the United States than land a Wienermobile Driver position. Applicants must have a good driving record, a taste for bad puns, and no shame.

The chosen few are sent for ten days of

keep going ➞

Spiked Rarebit

Suggestion: serve with

3 tablespoons butter
3 tablespoons flour
½ teaspoon dry mustard
1½ cups beer
1½ cups grated Cheddar cheese
¼ teaspoon paprika
¼ teaspoon grated nutmeg
dash of Worcestershire
pepper, to taste
4 hot dogs, sliced thin
4 English muffins, halved and toasted

1. In a medium saucepan, melt the butter. Stir in the flour and dry mustard and cook over low heat, whisking, for about 5 minutes.

2. Add beer and cook 10 minutes, whisking frequently.

3. Add remaining ingredients except the muffins and cook over low heat for 10 more minutes, stirring occasionally.

4. Serve on toasted English muffins.

Makes 4 servings.

indoctrination to Oscar Mayer headquarters in Madison, Wisconsin, where they get "grilled with questions" to see if they can "cut the mustard" and learn to pull out far enough around corners so that they don't scrape their buns on the curb. They also learn dis-

yep, keep going →

Sloppy Franks

Suggestion: serve with

½ cup finely chopped onion
½ cup finely chopped green pepper
2 tablespoons butter
1 8-ounce can tomato sauce
¼ teaspoon salt
½ cup barbecue sauce
¼ teaspoon pepper
½ tablespoon sugar
8 hot dogs, sliced
8 hamburger buns

1. Sauté onion and green pepper in butter until soft.

2. Stir in the tomato sauce, barbecue sauce, salt, pepper, sugar, and hot dogs.

3. Cook over very low heat for about 25 minutes, stirring frequently.

4. Serve over heated hamburger buns

Makes 8 servings.

creet vehicle behavior—"people know when the car is parked, for example, in front of a bar . . . there are no secrets, you can't hide in a Wienermobile."

The drivers stop by schools and grocery stores and sometimes escort couples from their weddings, featuring banners like "Just

a little more ➝

Cheese 'n Hot Dog Crescents

Suggestion: serve with 🍺

4 slices American cheese
8 hot dogs
1 8-ounce can refrigerated crescent dinner rolls

1. Cut four cheese slices into 6 strips each.

2. Slit hot dog to within $1/2$-inch of ends and insert 3 cheese strips.

3. Center hot dog on dinner roll and roll up. Place on a baking sheet cheese side up.

4. Bake at 375° for 12 to 15 minutes.

Makes 8 servings.

Linked" and "For Better or Wurst." A Wienermobile seats six and features a sunroof, microwave, refrigerator, cellular phone, and, best of all, a stereo system that can play "I wish I were an Oscar Mayer wiener" in twenty-one styles, from Cajun to rap to bossa nova.

THE END

A Coney Island

Suggestion: serve with 🍺

1 package cooked (boiled!) hot dogs
1 package hot dog buns
mustard
chili without beans (see below)
5 medium raw onions, chopped

Serve the hot dogs on buns with a swab of mustard, some chili, and a *hearty* sprinkling of the onions.

The Chili

6 tablespoons butter, margarine, or salad oil
6 medium onions, sliced
1½ pounds ground beef
3 20-ounce cans tomatoes
1 6-ounce can tomato paste
1 cup beer
1 tablespoon salt
½ teaspoon Tabasco
2–4 tablespoons chili powder
2 12-ounce cans whole kernel corn

To Make the Chili

1. Melt the butter, margarine, or oil in a large saucepan.

2. Add the onions and cook until tender but not brown.

3. Add the ground beef and cook until lightly browned, breaking up with a fork.

4. Add the tomatoes, tomato paste, beer, salt, Tabasco, and chili powder. Cover and simmer 45 minutes.

5. Add the corn and simmer 15 minutes longer.

Makes 10 to 12 servings.

Southern Fried Devil Dogs

Suggestion: serve with

1 tablespoon Crisco, melted
1 egg
½ cup milk
⅛ teaspoon red pepper
¼ teaspoon paprika
½ teaspoon dry mustard
½ teaspoon baking powder
½ teaspoon salt
¾ cup sifted flour
6–8 hot dogs
¼ cup fine bread crumbs
Crisco for deep frying

1. Blend 1 tablespoon Crisco, egg, and milk. Mix seasonings and baking powder with the flour and add to Crisco mixture.

2. Dip hot dogs into bread crumbs, then into flour-Crisco-egg batter.

3. Fry in deep Crisco heated to 365° (or when an inch cube of bread browns in 60 seconds) until brown. Drain on paper towels.

Makes 6 to 8 servings.

The Lonely Guy's Casserole

Suggestion: serve with

6 hot dogs, cut into bite-size pieces
1 20-ounce can pork and beans
¾ cup ketchup
½ cup water

1 tablespoon mustard
2 teaspoons Worcestershire
1 tablespoon brown sugar
4 scallions, chopped

Mix these ingredients well and put into a casserole.

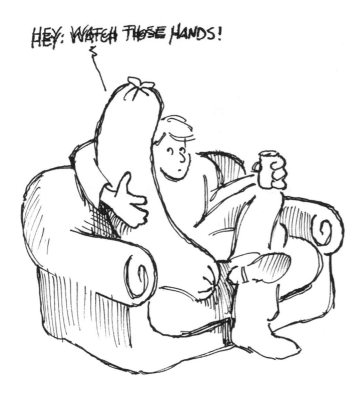

HEY, WATCH THOSE HANDS!

Cornbread Topping

¾ cup flour
1 tablespoon sugar
1½ teaspoons baking powder
1 teaspoon salt
⅔ cup cornmeal
1 beaten egg
⅔ cup milk
¼ cup cooking oil
⅓ cup minced onion

1. Sift flour, sugar, baking powder, and salt.

2. Stir in cornmeal. Add all at once to the dry ingredients the egg, milk, oil, and onion. Stir.

3. Spoon over bean mixture and bake at 400° for 35 minutes.

Makes 4 servings.

Hot Dog Canoes

Suggestion: serve with

12 slices soft white bread, crusts removed
½ cup melted butter
6 slices processed American cheese
2 tablespoons mustard
12 hot dogs

1. Brush one side of each slice of bread with the melted butter. Cut the slices of cheese into 4 equal strips and place a strip on the unbuttered side of the bread.

2. Brush the bread and cheese with the mustard. Place a hot dog on top of the cheese and bring up two opposite corners of the bread to meet on top of the hot dog. Fasten the bread in place with a toothpick.

3. Place on a cookie sheet in a 350° oven for 8 to 10 minutes, or until the bread has toasted to a crisp brown on the outside.

Makes 6 servings.

A VITAL FACT: the average number of hot dogs Americans eat in July is 1 billion.

Hot Dog Goulash

Suggestion: serve with plain boiled potatoes, crisp green salad, and 🍺 !

½ cup vegetable oil or shortening
6 large onions, coarsely chopped
2 cloves garlic, crushed
10 large green peppers, cut into 1½-inch cubes
1 tablespoon caraway seeds
2½ cups canned, undrained tomatoes
2 tablespoons paprika
salt and freshly ground black pepper, to taste
2 pounds hot dogs, sliced ½ inch thick

1. In a large heavy kettle, heat the oil and add the onions and garlic. Cook over moderate heat, stirring with a wooden spoon, until the onions begin to take on color.

2. Add the green peppers and cook, stirring, 5 minutes longer. Cover and continue cooking 20 minutes, stirring occasionally.

3. Add the caraway seeds, half the tomatoes, and the paprika and cover again. Simmer 20 minutes longer, stirring occasionally.

4. Add the remaining tomatoes, if necessary, to prevent the vegetables from becoming dry. When the goulash has thickened slightly, add the salt and pepper and hot dog slices. Cover and heat thoroughly.

Makes 6 to 8 servings.

Roadside Dogs

This is a great recipe!! It was inspired by my "second-favorite-of-all-time" cookbook— *Manifold Destiny: The One! The Only! Guide to Cooking on your Car Engine* by Chris Maynard and Bill Scheller. Boy, talk about attitiude and spirit—Chris and Bill's book is just like *The Hot Dog Cookbook* (my "absolute-all-time-favorite" cookbook). Imagine that! Two books with the same wonderful attitude! Some fancy book publisher should really look into a boxed set of the two…leather bound…gold leaf lettering…lots of very unhealthy publication parties, from Hollywood to New York…real high royalties…

Anyway, no serious cook's bookshelf should be without both *The Hot Dog Cookbook* and *Manifold Destiny*; and here's a wonderful example of why:

Suggestion: serve with 🍺 (but maintain a designated driver at all times)

10 hot dogs
American processed cheese, sliced into 10 hot-dog-length strips
10 slices bacon
10 hot dog buns

1. Cut a deep slit in each hot dog and stuff with the cheese.

2. Then diagonally (as if you're taping up a broken baseball bat with bacon) wrap each hot dog with a slice of bacon.

3. Wrap tightly with foil and jam these into various odd, but secure, places on your car's engine.

4. Start up your car and drive at about 60 miles an hour for 40 minutes, or until the cheese is melted and the bacon is somewhat crisp.

5. Pull over to the side of the road or into the parking lot at the company picnic or your in-laws' driveway, turn off the engine, remove the dogs from the foil, place in bun, garnish as you wish, and, remember, do not litter.

Makes 5 to 8 servings.

Hot Dog Open-Face Sandwiches

Suggestion: serve with

8 hot dogs
1 3-ounce package cream cheese, at room temperature
1 teaspoon Dijon mustard
¼ teaspoon horseradish
2 tablespoons milk
1 scallion, chopped fine
1 tablespoon chopped parsley
8 English muffins, cut in half and toasted
1 teaspoon paprika

1. Chop the hot dogs and mix with cream cheese, mustard, horse-radish, milk, scallion, and parsley.

2. Spread each English muffin half with the mixture and sprinkle with paprika.

3. Place on a cookie sheet and broil about 6 inches from the heat for 5 minutes or so, until the sandwiches begin to brown.

Makes 8 servings.

> "Gourmet is where you find it. A hot dog with relish is a ballpark gourmet food."
>
> —Vincent Price, actor and art connoisseur

Olé

Suggestion: serve with

8 hot dogs
1 10¼-ounce can jalapeño bean dip
8 tortillas (flour or corn, your call)
1 16-ounce can chili
1 cup grated Cheddar cheese
2 scallions, chopped

1. Split the hot dogs lengthwise, being careful not to cut all the way through, and spread the inside of each hot dog with a generous portion of the jalapeño bean dip. Set aside.

2. Warm each tortilla in a skillet. As soon as the tortilla begins to soften, remove and roll it around the bean-stuffed hot dog. Place in the bottom of a greased casserole dish.

3. Open the can of chili and spread over the tortillas. Sprinkle the top with cheese and scallions.

4. Bake in a 350° oven for 20 minutes or until the cheese has melted.

Makes 4 to 6 servings.

THE PERFECT HOT DOG

According to a random survey of "normal" Americans conducted by a *leading* hot dog processor, 48.3 percent of those surveyed consider the perfect hot dog to be six inches long, whereas 26 percent prefer the slightly longer seven-inch version, and, perhaps surprisingly, only 4 percent of normal Americans prefer foot-long hot dogs.

Surf 'n Turf

Suggestion: serve with

½ pound of deli-bought tuna salad
6 hot dog buns
6 cooked hot dogs

Spoon several tablespoons of tuna salad into a bun and lay a hot dog on top. Enjoy.

Makes 6 servings.

Creole Dogs

Suggestion: serve with

3 tablespoons margarine	½ teaspoon salt
¾ cup chopped onion	½ green pepper, cut into strips
1 16-ounce can tomatoes	8 hot dogs, cut into fourths
1 8-ounce can tomato sauce	¼ cup raisins
1 teaspoon chili powder	4 cups hot, cooked rice
2 teaspoons brown sugar	2 tablespoons parsley

1. Melt the margarine in a large skillet; add the chopped onion and sauté until soft.

2. Add the tomatoes and the tomato sauce. Stir well; add the chili powder, brown sugar, and salt. Continue to cook over low heat until it comes to a boil.

3. Add the green pepper strips, the pieces of hot dog, and the raisins. Reduce heat and simmer for 10 minutes or until the hot dogs are heated through.

4. Spread the rice on a heated platter and top with the hot dog mixture. Sprinkle wih parsley.

Makes 6 to 8 servings.

Marrakech Express

Suggestion: serve with rice and BEER

flour
1 medium eggplant, peeled and diced
1 large onion, chopped
2 cloves garlic, chopped
5 tablespoons oil
¼ teaspoon basil
salt and pepper, to taste
2½ cups canned tomatoes
1 teaspoon sugar
1 pound hot dogs, cut into 1-inch pieces

1. Put some flour in a plastic bag (about ¼ cup, I should say), add the eggplant, and toss it around until coated.

2. Sauté the onion and garlic in oil until onion is transparent.

3. Add the eggplant, salt and pepper, and basil and cook until eggplant is lightly browned.

4. Add the tomatoes and sugar and cook uncovered for 20 minutes or so, until some of the liquid has evaporated. Add the hot dogs and cook for about 10 more minutes.

Makes 4 servings.

Hawaiian Hots

Suggestion: serve with

½ cup diced green pepper

½ cup diced onion

1 tablespoon margarine

1 8-ounce can pineapple tidbits

¼ cup cider vinegar

2 tablespoons brown sugar

2 tablespoons soy sauce

large can pork and beans

6 hot dogs, sliced, then diced into quarters

1. In large skillet, sauté onion and green pepper in margarine until soft.

2. Add remaining ingredients and simmer for 15 minutes.

Makes 4 servings.

THE HEALTHY HOT DOG
Feature #2

Hot dogs contain protein, carbohydrates, fat, iron, thiamine, riboflavin, niacin, phosphorus, zinc, vitamin C, vitamin B_6, and vitamin B_{12}. These nutrients are all necessary to maintain healthy bodily functions.

The Hogan's Heroes Prune-and-Kraut Bake

Suggestion: serve with

2 1-pound cans sauerkraut

1 medium red apple

1 cup pitted prunes, cut into quarters

¼ cup grated onion

1 tablespoon dark brown sugar

8 hot dogs

3 cups mashed potatoes, seasoned with butter and salt
   and pepper

1. Drain the sauerkraut well; place in a mixing bowl; and slice (but don't peel) the apple. Add to the sauerkraut along with the quartered prunes, grated onion, and brown sugar. Mix and toss all together lightly.

2. Place in a baking dish. Arrange the hot dogs over the surface. Cover with foil and bake in a 350° oven for 25 minutes.

3. Remove the foil from the top and spoon the mashed potatoes around the edges. Return to the oven and bake for an additional 15 minutes or until the potatoes just begin to brown.

Makes 4 servings.

Dormitory Delight

Suggestion: BEER an absolute must!

1- or 2-cup dormitory coffeemaker (you know, like a metal cup
    with an electric cord-and-plug running out of it)
1 hot dog
1 slice generic white bread (Wonder Bread recommended)
1 or 2 single-serving pouches of ketchup (like you'd pick up at
    McDonald's or Burger King; check your coat pockets or car
    floor—there's usually one lying around somewhere)

1. Fill coffeemaker with water and cook the hot dog just long
   enough.
2. Wrap cooked hot dog with bread, garnish with ketchup, and
   enjoy.

Makes 1 serving.

FROM COW TO YOU
The Making of 1990s Hot Dogs

1. Selected meats are cut or ground into small pieces and placed in a mixer.

2. High-speed, stainless-steel choppers blend the meat, spices, and curing ingredients into a batter. This mixture is continuously weighed to assure a proper balance of all ingredients. ▪ ▪ ▪ ☞

Dog-A-Roni

Suggestion: serve with 🍺

8 ounces elbow macaroni
2 hot dogs
14 1/2-ounce can tomatoes
1 1/2 cups grated Cheddar cheese
1/4 cup grated Parmesan cheese
salt and pepper

1. Cook pasta until almost done (al dente); rinse and drain.

2. Heat oven to 350°.

3. Butter a 9-inch baking dish.

4. Slice hot dogs.

5. Drain tomatoes, reserving 1/2 cup juice, and chop.

6. Combine pasta, hot dogs, tomatoes, and reserved juice, 1/2 cup of the Cheddar, the Parmesan, and salt and pepper, to taste.

7. Place in casserole. Cover with foil and bake 45 minutes.

8. Remove foil and sprinkle with remaining Cheddar cheese. Bake, uncovered, 15 minutes longer.

Makes 4 servings.

3. The batter is then pumped into the old "automatic stuffer/linker" machine, where it's jammed into strands of cellulose casings. As the strands fill, they are automatically linked into hot dogs of an exact size and weight.

follow me 👉

Hot Dog Helper

Suggestion: serve with

1 pound frankfurters, cut in half diagonally
½ cup chopped onion
½ teaspoon basil or oregano leaves, crushed
2 tablespoons butter or margarine
1 can cream of celery or mushroom soup
½ cup milk
½ cup chopped canned tomatoes
2 cups cooked wide egg noodles
2 tablespoons chopped parsley

1. In skillet, brown frankfurters and cook onion with basil or oregano in butter until tender.

2. Stir in remaining ingredients. Heat; stir occasionally.

Makes 4 servings.

4. The linked strands are then moved by conveyor to the smokehouse, where they are fully cooked under controlled temperature and humidity conditions.

5. The hot dogs are next showered in cool water and fed through the old "high-speed automatic peeler" so that the cellulose skin is stripped away.

oh yes, there's more 👉

Stuffed Peppers

Suggestion: serve with 🍺

6 green or red peppers
4 hot dogs, chopped
2 cups cooked rice
$\frac{1}{2}$ cup frozen corn, thawed
$\frac{1}{2}$ cup grated Cheddar cheese
$\frac{1}{4}$ cup finely chopped scallions
1 teaspoon Worcestershire sauce

1. Cut a thin slice from the stem end of each pepper. Wash and remove all seeds and membrane. Place in a kettle with 1 cup water and cover and boil for 5 minutes. Drain.

2. Combine hot dogs, rice, corn, cheese, scallions, and Worcestershire sauce and mix well.

3. Fill peppers and bake in a 350° oven for about 25 minutes.

Makes 6 servings.

Classic Hot dogs

Suggestion: serve with

6 hot dogs
Cheez Whiz
6 strips bacon
6 hot dog buns

1. Slit the hot dogs lengthwise, being careful not to cut all the way through.

2. Squirt the Cheese Whiz inside each slit hot dog.

3. Fasten a strip of bacon to one end of the hot dog with a toothpick and spiral it around the cheese-filled hot dog. Fasten the other end of the bacon with another toothpick.

4. Place in the broiler and grill, turning the hot dogs until the bacon is crisp and golden on all sides.

5. Place the hot dogs in buns, remove the toothpicks, and serve.

Makes 6 servings.

7. Once packaged and boxed, the hot dogs are moved to storage coolers and loaded on refrigerated trucks for delivery to supermarkets, so that they may soon find their way into your breakfast nook and onto your picnic table.

The End!

Erb's Party Loaf

Suggestion: serve with 🍺

1 round loaf white bread
softened butter or margarine
Hot Dog and Celery Filling (see next page)
Curried Egg Filling (see next page)
2 tomatoes, thinly sliced
Avocado Filling (see next page)
½ pound cream cheese
light cream
sliced stuffed olives
fresh parsley sprigs

1. Cut loaf, crosswise, into four thick slices.

2. Spread each slice with butter.

3. Spread bottom slice with Hot Dog and Celery Filling. Top with second bread slice.

4. Spread with Curried Egg Filling. Top with slices of tomato and third bread slice.

5. Spread with Avocado Filling and top with remaining bread slice.

THE HOT DOG AS AN *INTERNATIONAL* PHENOMENON

In the key *mid-Atlantic state* of Maryland, at Frostburg State College, a 5,280-foot hot dog—long enough to wrap four times around a football field—was prepared in 1985.

6. Mash cream cheese; stir in enough cream so cheese will spread easily and beat until smooth. Spread the cream cheese on top and sides of the loaf. Garnish with olive slices and parsley. Cut into wedges to serve.

Hot Dog and Celery Filling: Combine 1 cup finely chopped (cooked) hot dogs, $1/2$ cup finely chopped celery, and enough mayonnaise to moisten.

Curried Egg Filling: Combine 4 finely chopped hard-cooked eggs, $1/2$ teaspoon curry powder, and enough mayonnaise to moisten.

Avocado Filling: Mash 2 fully ripe avocados; add 2 tablespoons seasoned French dressing. Stir until well blended.

Makes 8 servings.

A LOST OPPORTUNITY

When Joe Kremer, general manager of the Columbus (Georgia) minor league baseball team, went looking for a new team name that could bring in a lot of licensing revenue, he rejected "The Carolina Scramble Dogs" fearing that few people outside Georgia would know what "scramble dogs" meant: a chopped-up hot dog with chili and oyster crackers.

Valentine Dogs

Suggestion: serve with

12 cocktail franks
1 tablespoon butter or margarine
1 cup sugar
½ cup water
⅓ cup small red cinnamon candy hearts
6 cored apples, peels removed from top halves

1. Brown cocktail franks in 1 tablespoon butter or margarine.

2. Combine sugar, ½ cup water, and cinnamon candies and boil for 5 minutes.

3. Place apples peeled side down in the hot syrup and cook for 5 minutes.

4. Remove apples from syrup and place peeled side up in large baking pan.

5. Place 2 browned franks in center of each apple. Pour red cinnamon syrup over all.

6. Bake until tender, about 30 minutes at 350°.

Makes 4 servings.

Popeye's Dogs

Suggestion: serve with

10 hot dogs
2 10-ounce packages of frozen chopped spinach, cooked
    according to package directions and drained
1½ cups grated Cheddar cheese
1 garlic clove, minced
¼ teaspoon nutmeg
½ teaspoon Worcestershire
¾ cup instant rice
2 eggs, beaten
2 cups milk

MAJOR PLAYERS	
in the 1990s Hot Dog Biz	
Share of Market	
Oscar Mayer	12.8%
Ballpark	6.3%
Hygrade	4.1%
Bar S	3.9%
Louis Rich	3.7%

1. Slice hot dogs and place in buttered 10 x 8 x 2-inch baking dish.

2. Place the drained, cooked, chopped spinach in a large mixing bowl. Add the cheese, garlic, nutmeg, Worcestershire, and rice and mix well.

3. Add the eggs and milk to the spinach and rice mixture and pour over hot dogs.

4. Bake in 325° oven for 40 minutes, or until the center is firm to the touch.

Makes 8 to 10 servings.

Pat and Mike's Bickerson Special

Suggestion: serve with

6 pieces toasted white sandwich bread, buttered
4 or 5 hot dogs, sliced
2 tomatoes, sliced thin
6 slices Cheddar cheese
some Worcestershire

1. On toast, place slices of cooked hot dogs. Top with thin slices of tomato and slices of cheese.

2. Place under the broiler until hot and bubbly.

3. Top with a dash or two of Worcestershire.

Makes 6 servings.

If you cut hot dogs while they're still hot, they curl backwards, making for a ingenious and decorative dish. You can even stand them up on the curved legs, like a big old swamp tree with its roots working their way out of the ground. Top it off with a chunk of parsley and it really starts to look like a six-inch tree—enough to fool a toddler but never the neighbor's dog.

Pot Luck Supper

Suggestion: serve with

½ cup chopped celery

½ cup chopped onion

2 tablespoons margarine

1 pound frankfurters, cut in ½-inch slices

1 10 ¾-ounce can tomato soup

½ cup water

1 teaspoon Worcestershire sauce

½ box spaghetti, cooked and kept warm

1. Cook celery and onion in margarine until tender. Add frankfurters and cook until delicately browned.

2. Stir in soup, water, and Worcestershire and cook about 15 minutes to blend flavors, stirring often.

3. Serve over hot cooked spaghetti.

Makes 4 to 6 servings.

THE HOT DOG AS AN *INTERNATIONAL* PHENOMENON

In *Paris*, "le chien chaud" is enjoyed on lightly toasted French bread, served with Gruyere or Swiss cheese and enough hot Dijon mustard to bring tears to the eyes.

Frank 'n Spud Bake

Suggestion: serve with [beer bottle icon]

¼ cup chopped onion

1 tablespoon butter or margarine

1 can cream of celery soup

⅓ cup water

1 tablespoon prepared mustard

4 cups sliced cooked potatoes

6 hot dogs, sliced

1 cup grated Cheddar cheese

1. In saucepan, cook onion in butter until tender.

2. Stir in soup, water, and mustard and then toss in potatoes.

3. Pour into 1½-quart shallow baking dish and top with hot dogs, then cheese.

4. Bake in 400° oven for 25 minutes or until hot.

Makes 4 to 6 servings.

Be damn careful when feeding hot dogs to dogs!

There was a guy on Long Island who gave his mutt a hot dog fresh from the package. The mutt sucked down its treat, then suddenly gave its master a "what-the-hell" look, rolled up its eyes, and fell over dead.

The dog choked on the dog!

Hot Dog Cabbage Pie

Suggestion: serve with buttered noodles and

6 cups coarsely shredded cabbage

1/2 cup chopped onion

4 hot dogs

3 tablespoons brown sugar

3 tablespoons lemon juice

3 tablespoons butter

1/4 teaspoon caraway seeds

1. Cook cabbage 7 minutes in boiling, salted water. Drain and reserve liquid for soup another day.

2. Sauté onion until transparent in 1 tablespoon butter.

3. Place cabbage in a greased 9-inch pie plate. Slit hot dogs lengthwise, cut in halves crosswise and arrange attractively on bed of cabbage, cut side down.

4. Sprinkle with combined sugar and lemon juice. Dot with butter. Top with caraway seeds.

5. Bake in 400° oven about 10 minutes, or until hot dogs are browned and crusty.

Makes 4 servings.

> A really great thing about hot dogs is that they bug the hell out of vegetarians.

Diner Dinner

Suggestion: serve with

1 pound hot dogs, sliced

1½ cups corn chips, coarsely crushed

1 medium onion, chopped

1 cup grated sharp Cheddar cheese

1 16-ounce can baked beans

1 12-ounce can taco sauce

1. Divide all ingredients but taco sauce in half and layer twice in a casserole.

2. Top with sauce for tacos.

3. Bake at 300° for 45 minutes.

Makes 4 servings.

Hot Dogs and Broccoli Balls

Suggestion: serve with

1 envelope onion soup mix

2 cups hot water

2 10-ounce packages frozen broccoli balls (also known as brussels sprouts)

8 hot dogs

1 tablespoon dried parsley

1. Mix the onion soup and the hot water in a saucepan and add the broccoli balls. Cook until the balls are tender but not mushy.

2. Cut the hot dogs into 1-inch lengths and add to the broccoli balls. Turn the heat to very low and cook for 5 minutes. Turn off the heat and allow the hot dogs and the broccoli balls to stand in the hot liquid for another 5 minutes. *Don't cover.*

3. Drain off the liquid and throw away or save to make soup. Sprinkle the parsley over the sprouts and dogs. Mix lightly and serve immediately.

Makes 6 servings.

THE HOT DOG AS AN *INTERNATIONAL* PHENOMENON

In *Moscow,* the American-style hot dog is known as a *goriachie sobaki.*

Cabbage Rolls

Suggestion: serve with 🍺

1 3—4-pound head cabbage, with nice outside green leaves

3 cups boiling water

2 bay leaves

1 teaspoon garlic salt

¼ cup butter

1 cup chopped onion

12 hot dogs, chopped until the consistency of hamburger

⅔ cup instant rice, just as it comes from the package

½ cup sour cream

½ teaspoon salt

¼ teaspoon pepper

⅛ teaspoon nutmeg

2 cups canned tomato sauce

1. Remove 12 large outer leaves from the head of cabbage and wash them well. Place the leaves in a big pot with a tightly fitting cover and add the 3 cups of boiling water. Bring to a rollicking boil; then turn the heat to simmer, cover, and cook for about 5 minutes, or until the cabbage leaves are soft and tender. Drain and set aside.

There are over 3,000 licensed hot dog vendors in New York City, providing 13,000 jobs (including bakers, meat packers, delivery people, and pushcart manufacturers).

2. Cut the remainder of the cabbage into 4 wedges and shred. Place shredded cabbage over the bottom of a buttered 2-quart casserole with a tightly fitting cover. Add the bay leaves and sprinkle with the garlic salt. Set aside.

3. Melt the butter in a skillet, add the onion, and sauté until transparent. Add the chopped hot dogs and sauté until they begin to brown. Remove from heat and add the rice, sour cream, salt, pepper, and nutmeg and mix thoroughly.

4. Place about $1/4$ cup of the hot dog mixture on the stem end of a softened cabbage leaf. Roll toward the outer edge, tucking in the sides as you go along. Fasten tightly with a toothpick. Repeat with remaining cabbage leaves.

5. Place the stuffed cabbage rolls on top of the shredded cabbage in the casserole. Pour the tomato sauce over the rolls and the shredded cabbage. Cover tightly and place in a 325° oven for 45 minutes. Turn the cabbage rolls over and bake for an additional 15 minutes.

Makes 4 servings.

Sweet and Sour Dogs

Suggestion: serve with rice and

1 pound frankfurters, cut into 2-inch lengths
4 tablespoons oil
1 onion, coarsely chopped
1 green pepper, chopped
1 cup pineapple chunks with juice
2 small tomatoes, peeled, seeded, and quartered
2 tablespoons cornstarch
¼ cup dry vermouth
2 tablespoons white wine vinegar

1. Cook the hot dogs for 10 minutes in boiling water.

2. Heat the oil in a large skillet and add the onion, green pepper, pineapple and juice, and tomatoes. Cook until well blended and heated through.

3. Mix the cornstarch with a little water to make a paste and stir into the skillet with the vermouth and vinegar. Stir until smooth.

4. Mix in the drained hot dogs and simmer 5 minutes.

Makes 4 servings.

HELPFUL HINTS

● When looking for premium quality hot dogs, shoppers should read labels to look for a hot dog that is 100 percent pure beef and has no fillers or by-products, artificial ingredients or colors.

● If you're looking to save money or if you live in New Jersey (thus your health's probably already shot), ignore the above Helpful Hint.

Dog Biscuits

Suggestion: serve with

6 hot dogs
1 teaspoon powdered mustard
¼ cup pickle relish
1 egg, slightly beaten
¼ cup Heinz chili sauce
1 tube refrigerated baking powder biscuits

1. Chop the hot dogs coarse. Add the mustard, relish, egg, and chili sauce and mix thoroughly.

2. Flatten each half of the refrigerated biscuits until they are about 1 inch larger than they come in the can. Place some of the hot dog mixture in the middle of half the flattened biscuits. Moisten the outer edge with a little water. Press the top half of each biscuit onto the filling and seal the outer edges well.

3. Place each filled biscuit in a buttered muffin tin or on a buttered cookie sheet. Bake at 400° for 15 minutes, or until the biscuits are puffed up and golden brown.

Makes 4 servings.

THE HOT DOG AS AN *INTERNATIONAL* PHENOMENON

In *Canada,* at the Maple Lodge Farms in 1985, a 2,377-foot-long chicken hot dog was made.

Hot Dog Corn Fritters

Suggestion: serve with [beer bottle illustration]

6 eggs, separated
1 12-ounce can corn, drained
6 hot dogs, diced into $\frac{1}{4}$-inch pieces
$\frac{1}{2}$ cup all-purpose flour
$\frac{1}{2}$ teaspoon salt
1 tablespoon sherry

1. Beat the egg yolks until they are light and fluffy and add the corn, hot dogs, flour, salt, and sherry. Mix well.

2. Beat the egg whites until they stand in peaks. Gently fold the egg whites into the hot dog mixture.

3. Pour about $\frac{1}{4}$ of the mixture per fritter onto a hot, lightly oiled griddle and fry just like pancakes.

Makes 6 servings.

Cultural High-Brow and the Hot Dog

When Little, Brown and Company—one of the nation's oldest, largest, and most prestigious book publishers—published the memoirs of the very talkative talk show host Larry King, it built an entire marketing campaign around one simple quote of King's: *"There were no hot dogs in the world like Nathan's . . . a four-bite lunch that filled you up."*

Hot Dog Spaghetti Sauce

Suggestion: serve with spaghetti and

1 large onion, chopped

1 small green pepper, chopped

2 cloves garlic, chopped

4 tablespoons oil

1 28-ounce can crushed tomatoes

1/2 teaspoon basil

1/4 teaspoon oregano

1 teaspoon sugar

6 frankfurters, finely chopped

salt and pepper, to taste

1 small can tomato paste

1. Sauté the onion, green pepper, and garlic in the oil. Add the tomatoes, basil, oregano, and sugar. Bring to a boil, turn down the heat, and simmer uncovered for 20 minutes.

2. Add frankfurters, salt and pepper to taste, and the tomato paste and cook another 15 minutes.

Makes 4 srvings.

THE HEALTHY HOT DOG

Feature #3

Hot dogs are an excellent source of complete animal protein. Vegetable protein found in soybeans (blah!) and cereal grains (ugh!) is incomplete—*no vegetable contains the proper amounts of all the eight amino acids essential to human well-being.*

Creamed Hot Dogs

Suggestion: serve with rice or noodles and 🍺

1 pound hot dogs
1 small onion, chopped
2 tablespoons olive oil
1 cup ketchup
½ teaspoon brown sugar
1 cup heavy cream
salt and pepper to taste

1. Slice the hot dogs into ½-inch pieces.
2. Sauté the onion in the oil until lightly browned. Add the hot dogs and toss until heated through.
3. Add the ketchup and sugar and bring to a boil.
4. Stir in the cream and blend until smooth.
5. Simmer until thickened and add salt and pepper to taste.

Makes 4 servings.

THE HEALTHY HOT DOG

Feature #4

What is most important about eating hot dogs is making them a consistent part of a well-balanced daily menu.

Hot Dog and Beer Chili

Suggestion: serve with

2 16-ounce cans kidney beans, rinsed and drained
2 tablespoons chili powder or more, to taste
½ teaspoon Tabasco
¼ teaspoon red pepper flakes
½ cup beer
about 2 cups cut-up hot dogs
chopped green onions
grated Cheddar cheese

1. Throw the beans, chili powder, Tabasco, red pepper flakes, beer, and hot dogs into a largish pot and heat until hot.

2. Top each serving with chopped green onions and grated Cheddar.

Makes 4 servings.

> On the average the number of hot dogs sold at stadiums for sporting events averages about 80 percent of the attendance figures (sometimes hot dog sales even outnumber the spectators).

Klink's Hot Potato Salad

Suggestion: serve with

12 medium well-scrubbed red potatoes

3 hard-boiled eggs

1 pound wieners, sliced diagonally and heated through

2 slices bacon

1 teaspoon flour

½ cup vinegar

½ cup water

3 teaspoons sugar

salt and pepper, to taste

2 tablespoons chopped fresh parsley

1. Boil the potatoes in their skins until soft but not mushy. Cool a bit, then slice and place in serving bowl. Add sliced wieners and keep warm.

2. Chop 2 hard-boiled eggs and add to the potatoes.

3. Cut the bacon and fry until crisp. Add flour to bacon in pot and mix.

4. Mix the vinegar, ½ cup water, and the sugar. Add to the bacon and flour, stir, and let come to a boil.

5. Pour this over the potatoes, stir gently, and top with 1 chopped hard-boiled egg. Add salt and pepper to taste.

6. Top with fresh parsley.

Makes 8 servings.

Fat Tuesday Special

Suggestion: serve with

1 tablespoon oil

1 pound hot dogs, cut in ½-inch slices

½ green pepper, chopped

1 tablespoon flour

3 cups cooked shrimp

3 cups diced tomatoes (fresh or canned)

2½ cups water

1 large onion, sliced

2 cloves garlic, minced

4 tablespoons chopped parsley

2 cups uncooked rice

1¼ teaspoons salt

2 tablespoons Worcestershire sauce

½ teaspoon thyme

¼ teaspoon red pepper

chopped parsley for garnish

1. Heat oil in large skillet and add hot dogs and green pepper. Cook 5 minutes, stirring frequently.

2. Whisk in flour until smooth and cook 1 minute longer. Add shrimp, tomatoes, water, onion, garlic, and parsley.

3. Bring to a boil and stir in rice and all remaining ingredients except parsley. Cover and cook over low heat for 30 minutes, or until rice is tender and most of liquid is absorbed. Add water, if necessary.

4. Sprinkle with chopped parsley and serve.

Makes 6 servings.

New England Stuffed Tomatoes

Suggestion: serve with

6 large tomatoes
4 hot dogs, chopped
2 tablespoons butter or margarine
½ cup frozen corn, cooked
¼ cup scallions, including green tops, chopped
1 cup soft fresh bread crumbs
½ teaspoon sugar
1 teaspoon dried basil
salt and pepper, to taste

1. Slice tops from tomatoes, scoop out the centers, and place pulp in mixing bowl.

2. Sauté franks in butter until they begin to brown. Add the browned franks and remaining ingredients to tomato pulp and stuff the mixture into the tomatoes. Sprinkle with buttered bread crumbs, if desired.

3. Place in baking dish and bake at 350° for 30 minutes.

Makes 6 servings.

THE CELEBRITY HOT DOG

Rawley's, a drive-in located in Fairfield, Connecticut, which has been renowned around the world over the last forty-five years for its extraordinary hot dogs, counts among its customers the very rich and the very famous—such as Paul Newman, Dennis Quaid, Meg Ryan, Mike Wallace, Phil Simms, and Joe Namath.

Noodle Goulash

Suggestion: serve with

1 tablespoon butter or margarine

1 medium onion, chopped

1 cup chopped celery

½ pound hot dogs, sliced thin

8 ounces egg noodles

2½ cups canned chopped tomatoes

1 cup shredded Cheddar cheese

1 teaspoon sugar

1. Sauté onion and celery until onion becomes transparent. Add hot dogs and cook until lightly browned.

2. Cook noodles *al dente* in large saucepan and drain. Add all ingredients to noodles, mix gently, and place in buttered 2-quart casserole.

3. Bake at 350° for 45 minutes.

Makes 6 servings.

THE HOT DOG AS AN *INTERNATIONAL* PHENOMENON

In *Australia, Canada, The Philippines,* and *Japan,* hot dogs are most often enjoyed "American-style"—eaten in a soft bun with mustard and relishes.

Sally's Sufferin' Succotash

Suggestion: serve with

3 tablespoons oil

2 medium onions, chopped

2 green peppers, chopped

1 pound franks, chopped

2 cups creamed corn

2 cups lima beans, cooked

2 tomatoes, chopped

1 teaspoon sugar

1. In large skillet, heat oil and sauté onions and green peppers until they become soft.

2. Add franks and cook for a couple of minutes. Add remaining ingredients and simmer for 15 minutes or until tender.

Makes 4 servings.

HOT DOGS NOW TRENDY

In January 1992, Dave Jenkins, director of the NET (National Eating Trends) division of the NPD Group Inc., a major marketing research firm based in Port Washington, New York, revealed that analysts had determined that for the first time in six years Americans were less concerned about eating foods that contain supposedly unhealthy substances.

Potato Boats

Suggestion: serve with

4 large baking potatoes
1 small onion, chopped
4 hot dogs, chopped
4 tablespoons butter
2 tablespoons milk
½ cup grated Cheddar cheese
1 tablespoon minced fresh parsley

1. Prick the potatoes in a few places and bake at 450° for an hour or so until done.

2. Sauté onion and franks in 2 tablespoons of butter for 5 minutes or so, until the onion is transparent and the franks begin to brown.

3. Slice the potatoes in half lengthwise and let cool a few minutes. With a spoon, scoop the flesh into a large bowl.

4. Mash the potato with a fork, then stir in the remaining ingredients.

5. Scoop the mixture back into the potato shells and place on a baking sheet.

6. Bake 20 minutes or so, until hot and bubbly.

Makes 4 servings.

Judy's Hungry Gal Special

Suggestion: serve with brown bread and

1 pound hot dogs, sliced
1 16-ounce can baked beans
½ cup ketchup
½ cup chopped scallions
¼ cup brown sugar
½ teaspoon dry mustard
½ teaspoon Worcestershire

1. Combine all ingredients in large saucepan.
2. Simmer for 20 minutes or so until heated through and be sure not to invite the parents over.

Makes 4 servings.

The Legendary Mr. Nathan Handwerker

When my hero founded his very first "Nathan's Famous Coney Island Hot Dog Stand," people were dubious (remember, for the most part these were New Yorkers) of a sandwich that cost a mere five cents.

So Nathan hired a group of handsome, wholesome-looking young men, dressed them in starched white coats, put a stethoscope in each outside breast pocket with just enough of the instrument showing to iden-

go to the next page for the rest

Corny Bread

Suggestion: serve with

¾ cup flour

3 teaspoons baking powder

2 tablespoons sugar

½ teaspoon salt

¾ cup cornmeal

1 egg, beaten

6 tablespoons butter, melted

¾ cup milk

½ cup chopped hot dogs

1. Sift together dry ingredients. In separate bowl mix egg, 3 tablespoons of the butter and the milk.

2. Pour into sifted mixture and blend.

3. Pour into a greased 8-inch square pan. Bake at 425° for 15 minutes.

4. Remove from oven and quickly press chopped franks lightly into top of corn bread. Dribble remaining butter over top. Return to oven; bake 10 minutes.

Makes 6 servings.

tify the young man as possible intern or doctor. All these young men had to do for their wages was to cheerfully munch Nathan's five-cent wieners in front of his stand. Naturally, all those cynical New Yorkers took notice of these young wiener-munching "doctors" and figured that if the good doctors ate and liked these odd sandwiches, they just had to both taste good and be good for your health.

And thus the clever beginning of what is today globally recognized as a major culinary empire.

Frank 'n Stein

Suggestion: serve with 🍺

2 tablespoons oil
1 medium onion, chopped
3 cups sauerkraut, rinsed and drained
1 teaspoon caraway seeds
1 pound franks
12 ounces beer

1. Heat oil in large skillet and sauté onion until soft.

2. Add sauerkraut and caraway to skillet and mix well.

3. Place franks on top of heated mixture, pour beer over top.

4. Cover and simmer 20 minutes.

Makes 4 servings.

Cherry Cola
Franks and Beans

Suggestion: serve with

1 28-ounce can baked beans
1 pound hot dogs, sliced
1 bunch of scallions, finely chopped
1 green pepper, chopped
1 tomato, chopped
¼ cup dark brown sugar
⅓ cup cherry cola

1. Place baked beans and hot dogs in baking dish. Gently mix in scallions, green pepper, and tomato.

2. Combine sugar and cherry cola and pour evenly over bean mixture.

3. Bake, covered, at 350° for ½ hour.

Makes 4 to 6 servings.

> According to the National Hot Dog & Sausage Council, 95 percent of Americans serve hot dogs in their homes.

Hot Dog Burgers

Suggestion: serve with

½ pound ground beef

8 hot dogs, split lengthwise

1 8-ounce can tomato sauce

1 medium onion, finely chopped

1 clove garlic, minced

¼ teaspoon dry mustard

dash of Worcestershire

8 hot dog or hamburger buns

1. In a large skillet, cook beef until browned. Add franks, tomato sauce, onion, garlic, mustard, and Worcestershire and cook about 20 minutes, stirring frequently.

2. Serve in warmed hot dog or hamburger buns.

Makes 4 to 6 servings.

Barbecue Madness

"Backyard barbecues are America's contribution to the world of cuisine."
—*Family Circle*

"And hot dogs are the vital contribution to successful backyard barbecues."
—Jess M. Brallier

I really believe that. Most of us live with a modern, fully equipped kitchen, in a comfortable, bug-less, bird-less, smoke-less home free of wild dog packs. So why do we keep going outside with the chops, roasts, and steaks? Because it's more fun! It feels good. It's friendlier. And cooking weird food there doesn't smell up the house for days. So be sure to make it easy once you're out there. Don't let your beer go warm on you. Don't

risk undercooking the chicken. And don't burn a really expensive cut of prime beef. Stick to hot dogs. That's why, I'm sure, God had them invented.

If you burn the wieners, big deal (see page 105)! They don't cost that much; open up another pack, or stick the burnt dog in a bun and hide it under lots of condiments—nobody'll even know it's burnt, especially some little kid. And don't worry about undercooking them—dogs are already cooked (unlike really dangerous foods such as chicken). Best of all, hot dogs are easy to cook. You can drink beer, talk, and play horseshoes while cooking. That's great. Who was it anyway who declared that the host can't enjoy himself or herself?

One warning: Hot dogs can roll, like right off the grill and into the charcoal or onto the grass. So place them on those strips of metal carefully. Don't let go of the tongs or fork until the dogs come to a complete stop.

Foilproof (get it?) Wieners

Suggestion: serve with 🍺

wieners
foil
your choice of stuff
wiener buns

1. Place each wiener in double (really keeps the flies away) layers of foil and spread with *your choice of stuff*—like mustard, chopped onions or scallions, relish, cheese strips, or hey, use your imagination! Impress the nephews and nieces (I always do). Have fun! Summer's just too damn short anyway.

2. Wrap the foil tightly around each wiener and cook over coals for 10 minutes, turning once, then remove foil and serve wieners—including the condiments they cooked with—on toasted buns.

Makes 1 serving.

THE HOT DOG AS AN *INTERNATIONAL* PHENOMENON

At Camp David in 1970, Prince Charles and Princess Anne of the *British Commonwealth* feasted on barbecued hot dogs . . . . and the Royal Family's never been the same since.

Wienie Beanies

Suggestion: serve with 🍺

barbecue sauce
8 wieners, split
Boston baked beans
chopped red onion
8 buns

1. Spoon barbecue sauce over wieners and top with Boston baked beans and red onion.
2. Place wieners in aluminum foil and wrap tightly. Heat on coals for about 10 minutes. Remove foil and serve on toasted buns.

Makes 8 servings.

> "It is our destiny to do for hot dogs what McDonald's did for hamburgers . . . after all, whenever a presidential candidate visits New York, he invariably drops into Nathan's for a quick bite."
>
> — Wayne Norbitz, Nathan's president and chief executive, on its plans for expansion

Basic Backyard Barbecue

Suggestion: serve with 🍺

12 franks
mustard
ketchup
1 16-ounce can sauerkraut
6 toasted buns

1. For each serving, split 2 frankfurters lengthwise but not completely through. Spread one half of each frank with mustard and the other with ketchup. Arrange 3 to 4 tablespoons drained sauerkraut on one frankfurter, top with second frank, cut side down.

2. Fasten ends with wooden picks. Wrap in double-thickness aluminum foil.

3. Cook directly on hot coals 3 to 4 minutes on each side. Serve on toasted bun.

Makes 6 servings.

THE HOT DOG AS AN *INTERNATIONAL* PHENOMENON

In *Germany*, frankfurters are generally served with mustard and a hard roll.

Campfire Dogs

Suggestion: serve with BEER

8 dogs
1 25-ounce can chili
1 cup corn chips, crushed
8 buns

1. Split wieners lengthwise.

2. Combine chili and corn chips.

3. Spoon over wieners and place in buns.

4. Wrap in double-thickness aluminum foil and grill for 10–15 minutes.

Makes 8 servings.

PROGRESS!

It was not that long ago that the entire process of manufacturing a hot dog—from meat trimmings to ready-for-the-happy-consumer's supper table—required nine hours, but now it takes about forty-five minutes at most.

Jimmy's Louisiana Black Dogs

(a.k.a. "What to Do When You've Burned the Wieners" . . . which *always* happens!)

Suggestion: serve with root beer *

12 dogs
12 buns
lots of toppings

1. Set dogs on grill and cook until thoroughly blackened (burnt!).
2. Place dogs on buns, bury them under a heap of toppings, and serve to unsuspecting children.

Makes 12 servings.

* This recipe is a guaranteed success with kids. Neighborhood moms will be calling you for the recipe. Try it!

ATTENTION CALORIE COUNTERS!

A hot dog and bun with condiments has the same amount of proteins, and no more calories than, a healthful eight-ounce cup of low-fat, flavored yogurt.

Bastes

Suggestion: serve with

some dogs
some horseradish and brown sugar *or* some pineapple preserves
some buns

1. Make diagonal cuts in frankfurters, not cutting completely through.

2. Cook 10–15 minutes, turning frequently, until franks are heated through. While cooking, brush liberally with your choice of either 1 part horseradish and 2 parts brown sugar, or pineapple preserves. Then serve on toasted buns.

The United States Department of Agriculture officially recognizes the following as legitimate names for the hot dog:

(1) wiener
(2) frankfurter
(3) frank
(4) furter

Purple Plum Franks

Suggestion: serve with

½ cup plum preserves
1 tablespoon lemon juice
¼ teaspoon ginger
8 franks
8 toasted buns

1. Combine preserves, lemon juice, and ginger in saucepan; simmer 5 minutes, stirring constantly.

2. Make diagonal cuts ¼ inch deep in each frankfurter. Grill, turning franks and basting frequently with plum mixture. Serve dog on bun.

Makes 8 servings.

> **"Laws are like hot dogs. It's better not to see them being made."**
>
> — Alice Winkle

Franny's Favorite Backyard Fillings

Suggestion: serve with

For each serving, fry 1 strip of bacon for 2 minutes on each side. Split frankfurter lengthwise, not cutting completely through. Place your fillings in the cut and wrap with bacon. Secure with wooden toothpicks and fire up the grill. These can be enjoyed in a toasted bun or *sans* bun.

Bali Hai Franks: Place pineapple spears and chopped macadamia nuts in cut.

Meloned Franks: Place cantaloupe spear in cut.

Oriental Franks: Place 3 mandarin orange segments in cut.

Green Onion Franks: Place scallion in cut.

Franks 'n Mushrooms: Place 3 pickled mushrooms in cut.

Franks 'n Pickles: Place thin dill pickles in cut.

Blue Cheese Franks: Place crumbled blue cheese (that's why they're called "blue cheese franks") in cut.

THE HOT DOG AS AN *INTERNATIONAL* PHENOMENON

In 1976, the grand *eastern seaboard* city of Philadelphia celebrated the American Bicentennial with the unveiling of a five-foot-long, 1,776-ounce hot dog.

Screwy Louie Kabobs

Suggestion: serve with 🍺

12 franks, each cut into 3 or 4 pieces
24 whole mushrooms
2 large green peppers, cut into 1½-inch squares
24 pineapple chunks
1 cup molasses barbecue sauce (see below)

1. Thread franks, vegetables, and pineapple, alternately, onto skewers.

2. Baste generously with barbecue sauce.

3. Grill 5 to 6 inches above the hot coals, 3 to 4 minutes on each side. Brush with sauce several times during cooking.

Makes 8 servings.

Basic Molasses Barbecue Sauce

¼ cup cornstarch
4 cups lemon juice
2 cups oil
12 ounces molasses
2 tablespoons salt
1 tablespoon black pepper
6 cloves garlic, minced

1. Combine cornstarch and lemon juice in a saucepan. Cook and stir over low heat until mixture bubbles and thickens. Cool.

2. Using hand-held or electric beater, beat in remaining ingredients until thoroughly blended and thickened.

3. Store in refrigerator until needed. Makes 2 quarts.

Frank Lin Delanos

Suggestion: serve with 🍺

½ cup soy sauce
⅓ cup ketchup
¼ cup olive oil
¼ cup cider vinegar
1 teaspoon prepared horseradish
½ teaspoon dry mustard
¼ teaspoon thyme
12 hot frankfurters
buns optional

1. Combine first seven ingredients to make a marinade.
2. Cut gash in franks and cover with marinade. Refrigerate for 4 hours.
3. Drain and reserve marinade.
4. Put franks on grill and cook about 10 minutes, turning often and basting with reserved marinade. These can be enjoyed with or without a toasted bun.

Makes 6 servings.

The Milwaukee hot dog, essentially a bratwurst sausage, and the city's Secret Stadium Sauce have earned fans from around the world. Secret Stadium Sauce is in such demand that it's now bottled in pints and offered at nearly 200 supermarkets and specialty

Crunch 'n Franks

Suggestion: serve with 🍺

6 franks
⅓ cup bottled barbecue sauce
1 cup finely crushed garlic potato chips
6 buns

1. Coat each frank with barbecue sauce and then roll in the chips. Let stand for 30 minutes to set (like you'd let plaster set before painting it).

2. Grill about 4 inches from the coals, about 2 minutes on each side, or until coating is browned and the franks are hot.

3. Serve in buns; breathe lightly.

Makes 6 servings.

stores. Bob Costas, the award-winning (thus, no dummy he) NBC sportscaster, announced on a network telecast from Milwaukee's County Stadium, "Coming here and especially eating here—forget about the ball game—approaches a religious experience."

South of the Border Francos

Suggestion: serve with 🍺

2 pounds franks
16 tortillas
1 16-ounce can refried beans, heated
1 cup shredded Cheddar cheese
sliced green onions

1. Grill franks for about 10 minutes, until bubbly hot.

2. While franks cook, heat tortillas on grill, turning with tongs.

3. Place franks in tortillas and top with refried beans, cheese, and green onions. Roll up and serve.

Makes 16 servings.

The great social and cultural critic, H.L. Mencken, on the vital need for this book . . .

"In place of the single hot dog of today there should be a variety as great as that which has come to prevail among sandwiches. There should be hot dogs for all appetites, all tastes, all occasions. They should come in rolls of every imaginable kind and be accompanied by every sort of relish, from Worcestershire sauce to chutney. The hot dog should be elevated to the level of an art form."

—H.L. Mencken (1929)

Crown Roast of Hot Dogs

Whatever you do, don't limit your reading to *Esquire, The New Yorker,* and *Southern Review.* I came across this recipe, probably my all-time favorite (surely more so than even some of Mom's) in an old, out-of-print book entitled *Family Circle's Outdoor Cooking.* So stay tuned for old books at flea markets and yard sales, even attics when you're poking around at those Sunday open houses real estate agents always have.

Suggestion: serve with

2 1-pound packages hot dogs

1 stick margarine

1 large onion

1 loaf (1 pound) sliced white bread, cut into small cubes

2 teaspoons salt

1 teaspoon dried basil

½ cup hot chicken broth

1 can (12 or 16 ounces) whole kernel corn

2 pimientos, diced

¾ cup light corn syrup

3 tablespoons prepared yellow mustard

1. Thread a trussing or crewel needle with cotton twine, not thread. Insert needle lengthwise through center of frankfurters to make a long chain of hot dogs; knot twine at

ends to make a circle. Place on a circle of aluminum foil cut to fit "crown" on a metal pizza pan.

2. Melt margarine in a large saucepan. Sauté onion in margarine until soft and stir in bread cubes, salt, and basil until evenly coated with onion butter mixture. Pour in chicken broth and toss with a fork until blended. Add corn and liquid and pimientos and toss.

3. Pile stuffing inside hot dog "crown." Brush frankfurters generously with mixture of corn syrup and mustard.

4. Grill, 5 inches from the heat, with grill covered, basting several times with mustard mixture, 40 minutes, or until hot dogs are glazed and stuffing is piping hot. Slide onto serving platter with a pancake turner. And be sure not to serve or eat any of the twine.

Makes 8 to 10 servings.

Loaf o' Franks on a Grill

Here's another one I can't take credit for. It, too, was discovered in an old, out-of-print yard-sale find entitled *Culinary Arts Institute, The Outdoor Cookbook* (don't let the "Culinary Arts Institute" put you off—this recipe can be enjoyed just like really tacky yard sales and the rest of this book).

Suggestion: serve with

8 frankfurters

½ cup shredded sharp Cheddar cheese

3 tablespoons finely chopped mushrooms

3 tablespoons finely chopped pitted green olives

2 tablespoons finely chopped onion

2 tablespoons ketchup

2 garlic cloves, minced

½ teaspoon Worcestershire sauce

½ teaspoon salt

¾ cup butter or margarine

¾ teaspoon dry mustard

1 loaf French bread

2 teaspoons sesame seeds

1. Make a lengthwise slit almost through each frankfurter. Mix cheese and the next seven ingredients. Fill each frankfurter and set aside.

2. Cream butter and mustard together and set aside.

3. Use an apple corer to diagonally cut holes about 1 1/2 inches in diameter and 1 inch apart into sides and through the loaf of bread.

4. Spread cavities with about a third of the mustard butter. Insert filled frankfurters, allowing ends to extend equally from each side. Spread about a quarter of remaining mustard butter on the bottom of loaf and remainder on top. Top with sesame seeds.

5. Wrap loaf in heavy-duty aluminum foil and seal tightly. Place loaf to one side of grill over warm, not hot, coals. Grill 30 to 40 minutes, or until frankfurters are heated and bread is crisp. Turn several times.

6. To serve, unwrap and slice loaf between frankfurters.

Makes 8 servings.

Campfire Dogs

Suggestion: serve with

hot dogs
1 long green stick per person
buns

1. Get a good campfire going.

2. Peel the bark from a long (at least arm's length), green stick.

3. Once the fire dies down a bit, poke the sticks through the hot dogs and cook slowly near the fire.

4. Place on buns and eat.

5. Sing a stupid song (like "Kum-Ba-Ya").

**THE HOT DOG
AS AN
INTERNATIONAL
PHENOMENON**

In *Brazil*, the American-style hot dog is known as a *chucharro querte*.

Feeding the Masses

Hot dogs are just perfect when you've been stuck with having the factory over for the end-of-the-summer Labor Day bash. Hot dogs are true red-white-and-blue American, so you don't risk offending anybody, from management to union agitators. They're also cheap, which is great because if everybody pitches in a reasonable amount of cash, you might even clear a sizable profit (my uncle put one of my cousins through college just by hosting company, church, and block parties and serving—mind, this is the key!—*hot dogs*). Also, kids love hot dogs. There's nothing worse than the boss's obnoxious kid starting to scream about the food just as you're on the end of the diving board, ready to show off the back flip you've been working on all summer.

Some experts claim that hot dogs are at their very best, that they really hit their stride, when prepared and served in massive quantities. Here's hoping that after trying the following, you'll find it difficult to disagree with them (which is why they're called "experts").

NEXT.

HOT DOGS

119

Frankfurters and Sauerkraut

Suggestion: serve with ![beer bottle] (maybe a keg)

10 pounds sauerkraut
10 pounds frankfurters (approximately 100)

1. Cook sauerkraut in juice and water for 1 hour.
2. Place sauerkraut and frankfurters in pans (11 inches x 19 inches x 2 1/4 inches).
3. Bake at 300° for 1/2 hour.

Makes 50 servings.

Frankfurters in Beer

Suggestion: go ahead and serve with ![beer bottle] anyway

100 frankfurters
8 quarts domestic beer

1. Cover frankfurters with beer.
2. Simmer slowly for 30 minutes.

Makes 50 servings. Recipe may be doubled.

Hot Dog Hamburgers

Suggestion: serve with 🍺

15 pounds ground beef

4 eggs, beaten

2 cups fine dry bread crumbs

1/4 cup minced onion

1/4 cup finely chopped parsley

1/2 cup ketchup

3 tablespoons salt

1 teaspoon pepper

1 1/2 pounds frankfurters, sliced

48 hot buttered hamburger buns

1. Combine ground beef, eggs, crumbs, onion, parsley, ketchup, garlic, and seasonings. Mix thoroughly and shape into 48 patties.

2. Cut each frankfurter into about 15 to 16 slices. Broil hamburgers on one side.

3. Flip burgers and press 4 to 5 frankfurter slices on top of each patty. Finish broiling. Serve on hot buttered buns.

Patties may be baked rather than broiled, which eliminates that darn flipping. Bake in 375° oven about 20 minutes, siphoning off any excess fat during baking.

Makes 48 servings.

Toppings

"Toppings are to hot dogs what honeymoons are to weddings."

—Brad Smith

Hot dogs may be grilled, broiled, pan fried, or boiled, and they take only minutes to cook. To enjoy them fully, the roll should be toasted: smear butter or margarine on each side of the open hot dog roll and run under the broiler. Fill each roll with a cooked hot dog and top with mustard, ketchup, chili, relish, piccalilli, or one of these special toppings.

And remember, serve with beer.

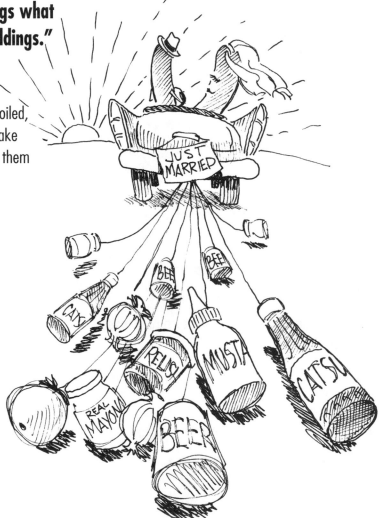

Toppings for Grilled Dogs

Suggestion: serve with 🍺

some dogs
some buns
and some stuff (see below)

You are to your grill what a mad scientist is to the heavily funded university lab. Here, as we move into toppings, is a real chance to let the imagination run loose. Start with the following to develop a rudimentary knack for what *stuff* works with wieners.

● Line toasted buns with home fries, place wieners on top, and finish off with ketchup.

● Spoon cole slaw onto buns and top with grilled wieners.

● Spread canned onion rings and corn relish over grilled wieners.

● Top wieners with chopped peanuts and tomato slices.

● Spoon cranberry relish over grilled turkey wieners.

● Line toasted wiener buns with 3-bean salad (store-bought will do the trick), put grilled wieners in, and top with mustard.

● Spoon a mixture of chili sauce and chopped red and green peppers over grilled wieners.

● Top grilled wieners with mashed avocado and crushed corn chips.

● Spread peach preserves on grilled wieners and top with mango chutney.

Hot Stuff Hot Sauce

Suggestion: serve with

1 tablespoon light brown sugar
2 tablespoons lemon juice
¼ cup molasses
2 tablespoons prepared mustard
2 teaspoons Worcestershire sauce
1½ teaspoons Tabasco
2 teaspoons chopped green onion

Using a saucepan, mix ingredients and simmer for 8 to 12 minutes, until it looks like you think it ought to.

Makes enough.

MUSTARD remains the most popular hot dog topping, being used regularly by 87.6 percent of Americans.

Dear Old Mom's Relish

3 cups chopped cucumbers

1½ cups chopped celery

⅓ cup chopped green or red pepper

1 cup chopped onions

4 tablespoons salt

2 cups spring water

1½ cups vinegar

½ cup sugar

1 teaspoon mustard seed

1 teaspoon celery seed

1. Put cucumbers, celery, green peppers, and onions into a mixing bowl (a bowl from the late 50s or early 60s tends to bring the right spirit to the situation).

2. Add the salt and water and let stand for at least 1 hour.

3. Then drain vegetables thoroughly, put in saucepan, and add remaining ingredients. Simmer for 5 minutes. Refrigerate.

Makes 3 pints.

A HOT DOG QUIZ

Q. According to the theme song from "The Patty Duke Show," what makes Patty lose control?

A. You guessed it, a hot dog!

Mayonnaise and Barbecue Sauce

1 cup store-bought (don't waste homemade on this!) mayonnaise
6 tablespoons barbecue sauce (again, store-bought)

Mix both ingredients well in a bowl (a yellow or green Russel Wright looks especially smashing).

Makes about 1 cup and 6 tablespoons of the sauce.

Chili, Chili Sauce

1 cup store-bought chili sauce
1 4-ounce can chopped mild green peppers

Combine ingredients and mix by hand (this doesn't really mean your *hand,* like your fingers and thumb—hell, you can be holding on to a fork or a spoon, for example—it just means don't use some machine like a blender); sauce should be chunky when served.

Makes a bit more than 1 cup.

Wiener Remoulade

1⅓ cups mayonnaise (store-bought or
    homemade)
1 small onion, chopped
¼ cup sweet pickle relish
2 tablespoons ketchup
1 tablespoon chopped fresh parsley (or
    ½ tablespoon dried)
1 tablespoon prepared mustard
1 tablespoon sugar

Put all this stuff in a bowl and mix well;
sauce should be chunky (if not, serve anyway . . . nobody will know the difference
unless I'm there).

Makes enough for 24 hot dogs.

Marlon's Sweet-and-Romantic Tahitian Sauce

1 cup apricot preserves
½ cup crushed/smashed tomatoes, drained
¼ cup sherry (or up to ½ cup depending on
    whom you're serving)
1 tablespoon oil
2 tablespoons soy sauce
3 tablespoons honey
½ teaspoon ground ginger

Combine everything in a saucepan and simmer for 8 to
12 minutes. Spoon over franks in buns (that's the way
Marlon likes it).

Quick 'n Easy, Down 'n Dirty Chili Sauce

1 large can chili with beans (cheapest can in the store—watch out for the
    expensive brands)
⅓ cup ketchup
¼ cup minced onion
1½ teaspoons chili powder
1 tablespoon brown sugar
½ teaspoon dry mustard

Put everything in a saucepan, mix, then simmer for 12 minutes (be sure to stir it every so often). Serve on hot dogs (this calls for your favorite brand!) and buns.

Makes enough for 8 hot dogs.

Curried Fruit Relish
(Faux Chutney)

1 8-ounce can crushed pineapple (packed in juice)
¼ cup brown sugar
2 tablespoons vinegar
½ teaspoon curry powder
⅛ teaspoon garlic powder
2 large unripe pears, peeled, cored, and chopped

1. Mix the pineapple and its juice, brown sugar, vinegar, curry powder, and garlic powder in a saucepan.

2. Bring to a boil and add the pears. Simmer uncovered for 8 minutes or until fruit is tender and relish is the desired—in the spirit of "to each, his or her own"—consistency.

3. Refrigerate, securely covered.

Makes about 1 cup.

List of Recipes

About the Author

JESS M. BRALLIER is a decent book publisher, occasional author, and major figure in the world of hot dogs. He admits that while some husbands sneak off for a secret drink or tryst, he sneaks out on his vegetarian wife to grab a hot dog.

He is the author of the bestselling *Lawyers and Other Reptiles* and the co-author of *The Pessimist's Journal of Very, Very Bad Guys; The Really Really Classy Donald Trump Quiz Book;* and *Write Your Own Living Will*.

Brallier, who has a cholesterol problem, is a native of Ligonier, Pennsylvania, and currently resides in Reading, Massachusetts, with his wife, Sally Chabert, and their two children, Max and Ruby.